Intellectual Property Law in Macedonia

Intellectual Property Law in Macedonia

Goce Naumovski
Maja Kambovska

This book was originally published as a monograph in the International Encyclopaedia of Laws/Intellectual Property Law.

Founding Editor: Roger Blanpain
General Editor: Frank Hendrickx
Volume Editor: Hendrik Vanhees

Wolters Kluwer

Published by:
Kluwer Law International B.V.
PO Box 316
2400 AH Alphen aan den Rijn
The Netherlands
E-mail: lrs-sales@wolterskluwer.com
Website: www.wolterskluwer.com/en/solutions/kluwerlawinternational

Sold and distributed by:
Wolters Kluwer Legal & Regulatory U.S.
7201 McKinney Circle
Frederick, MD 21704
United States of America
E-mail: customer.service@wolterskluwer.com

ISBN 978-94-035-0786-6

e-Book: ISBN 978-94-035-0996-9
web-PDF: ISBN 978-94-035-1006-4

The Authors

Dr Goce Naumovski holds an LLB, LLM and PhD in Legal Sciences from the Ss. Cyril and Methodius University in Skopje and a PhD in Intellectual Property Law/Private Law from the Centre for International Intellectual Property (CEIPI) at the University of Strasbourg. The title of his dissertation was: Relations Between Quality of Trademarks and Cognitive and Conative Variables of Consumers. He is a professor at the Faculty of Law 'Iustinianus Primus' of the Ss. Cyril and Methodius University in Skopje, where he has been teaching Trademark Law, Patent Law, Information Technology Law, Sports Law and related disciplines. In 2009, he was a visiting scholar at the Kernochan Center for Law, Media, and the Arts at Columbia University in New York.

Professor Naumovski was co-chair of the Double Degree LLM/DU programme of Intellectual Property Law, jointly organized by the Ss. Cyril and Methodius University and the University of Strasbourg, with the participation of professors from the European Intellectual Property Institutes Network (EIPIN) and universities from the region of Southeast Europe which included students from Macedonia, Bulgaria, Serbia, Greece, Albania, Kosovo, France, USA, Russia, Mexico, Armenia, Sweden, Nigeria and other countries.

He is a member of the International Association for the Advancement of Teaching and Research in Intellectual Property (ATRIP), the Lex Sportiva Sports Law Association, the Argumentum Research Association, etc.

Dr Naumovski actively participates in the Pan-European Seal Programme of the EPO and EUIPO. He participated in the EU Commission Tempus projects: 'Regional Postgraduate Studies in Intellectual Property Law'; 'EU-Industrial Property Law-Institution Building'; and 'Towards EU Standards in Copyright and Related Rights'. He was one of the founders of the Center for Intellectual Property Education in Skopje since its establishment.

He regularly participates in several international professional and scientific conferences and realizes study stays, including: WIPO/WTO Colloquium for Teachers of Intellectual Property; Commercial Law Development Program/Intellectual Property Program of the US Patent and Trademark Office; at the Center for International Intellectual Property Studies (CEIPI), University of Strasbourg, France; at the University of 'Macedonia' in Thessaloniki, Greece; Sofia University St. Kliment Ohridski and others.

He is the author or co-author of over eighty scientific and professional papers, many of which are in the field of intellectual property law.

Dr Naumovski is fluent in English, Greek, French, Croatian, Serbian, Bulgarian, Albanian and Latin.

Dr Maja Kambovska holds a PhD in Legal Sciences from Ss. Cyril and Methodius University in Skopje. Her doctoral dissertation was titled 'Copyright in the EU and in the Republic of Macedonia: Challenges in the Digital Environment'. She holds an LLM in EU Law from the College of Europe in Bruges, with a master's thesis in the field of EU and comparative intellectual property law. Prior to that, she finished her LLB studies in Skopje with a GPA of 10.00 (on a scale of 6–10), graduating as the best student in the class.

Dr Kambovska has extensive intellectual property and EU law and policy experience. She works at Roche Macedonia as a healthcare system partner, focusing on addressing systemic policy issues and engaging with stakeholders in pharmaceuticals and healthcare.

Her past career includes working for several years at the IFPI European Office in Brussels, where in her capacity as senior legal advisor she participated in discussions, consultations, and stakeholder forums with the EU institutions, other industry associations and stakeholders on EU legislative and other policy initiatives in the fields of intellectual property, e-commerce, digital single market, and other topics. She participated in the EU Commission Tempus project: 'Regional Postgraduate Studies in Intellectual Property Law'.

She has experience teaching Intellectual Property Law at FON University in Skopje, and is a Lecturer in Digital Copyright at the Double Degree LLM/DU IP law graduate programme jointly organized by the Ss. Cyril and Methodius University and University of Strasbourg. She has been engaged as a legal consultant on projects for legislative drafting and harmonization of the national laws with the EU acquis, in particular laws in the field of IP, trade and economy. Dr Kambovska has authored several publications on intellectual property law, digital policies, EU law and legislative harmonization, and has participated in numerous international scientific conferences and events.

Dr Kambovska is fluent in English, French, Serbian and Croatian.

Table of Contents

List of Abbreviations

CL	Law on Copyright and Related Rights
CrC	Criminal Code
EPC	European Patent Convention
EPO	European Patent Organisation
LARD	Law on Agriculture and Rural Development
LCM	Law on Customs Measures for Protection of Intellectual Property Rights
LCP	Law on Consumers' Protection
LIP	Law on Industrial Property
LPC	Law on the Protection of Competition
LQAP	Law on Quality of Agricultural Products
LTC	Law on Trade Companies
PCT	Patent Cooperation Treaty
SOIP	State Office of Industrial Property
WCGO	Wine with Controlled and Guaranteed Origin
WCO	Wine with Controlled Origin
WGI	Wine with Geographical Indication
WIPO	World Intellectual Property Organization
WTO	World Trade Organization

List of Abbreviations

Preface

The monograph includes an analysis of the primary and secondary legislation on intellectual property present in Macedonian legislation, i.e., laws, by-laws, regulations, and other sources regarding copyright and neighbouring rights, trademarks, trade names, industrial designs, plant variety protection, chip protection and geographical indications and appellations of origin. The monograph also includes references to the international conventions and agreements and relevant EU legislation documents, having in mind the EU Candidate status of the country. The authors' considerations and research references regarding the protection and enforcement of intellectual property rights are also part of this monograph.

General Introduction

§1. General Background

I. Geography

1. R.N. Macedonia is located in southern Europe on the Balkan Peninsula at latitude 41.608635 and longitude 21.745275. The country borders include 748 km (465 miles) of frontiers, shared with Serbia (62 km or 39 miles) to the North, Kosovo (159 km or 99 miles) to the northwest, Bulgaria (148 km or 92 miles) to the east, Greece (228 km or 142 miles) to the south, and Albania (151 km or 94 miles) to the west.

2. Having a central geographical position in the Balkans, the country is an intersection of key roads which have historically linked the east and the west. The area of the country is f 25,713 square kilometres. There are five mountains higher than 2,500 meters: Korab (2,864 meters), Sar (2,747 meters), Baba (2,601 meters), Jakupica (2,540 meters) and Nidze (2,521 metres). Almost 80% of the country's territory is mountains, plains include 19.1% and waters just 1.9%. The Macedonian rivers pertain to three basins, the Aegean, the Adriatic, and the Black Sea. Vardar, the largest river in this basin, drains 80% of the territory or 20,459 square kilometres (7,899 sq miles). Besides Vardar, other major rivers are: Crna, Bregalnica, Crni Drim, Pcinja, Treska, Strumica, Lepenec and Kriva Reka. There are three major lakes: Lake Ohrid, Lake Prespa and Lake Dojran.

3. The northern and western parts of the country are relatively close to a continental climate and the southern and eastern to a Mediterranean climate. There are four distinct seasons with warm and dry summers and moderately cold winters with heavy snowfall. The range of temperatures recorded throughout the year ranges from –20°C (–4°F) in winter, to 40°C (104°F) in summer. On average, there are three hundred sunny days per year, while the average annual precipitation is around 700 mm per year.

4. Concerning the administrative division, the country has seventy municipalities (opstini) and the capital city of Skopje as a special unit: Aracinovo, Berovo, Bitola, Bogdanci, Bogovinje, Bosilovo, Brvenica, Caska, Centar Zupa, Cesinovo-Oblesevo, Cucer Sandevo, Debar, Debarca, Delcevo, Demir Hisar, Demir Kapija, Dojran, Dolneni, Gevgelija, Gostivar, Gradsko, Ilinden, Jegunovce, Karbinci, Kavadarci, Kičevo, Kočani, Konce, Kratovo, Kriva Palanka, Krivogastani, Krusevo,

Kumanovo, Lipkovo, Lozovo, Makedonska Kamenica, Makedonski Brod, Mavrovo i Rostusa, Mogila, Negotino, Novaci, Novo Selo, Ohrid, Pehcevo, Petrovec, Plasnica, Prilep, Probistip, Radoviš, Rankovce, Resen, Rosoman, Sopiste, Staro Nagoricane, Stip, Struga, Strumica, Studenicani, Sveti Nikole, Tearce, Tetovo, Valandovo, Vasilevo, Veles, Vevcani, Vinica, Vrapciste, Zelenikovo, Zelino, and Zrnovci.

II. Cultural Composition

5. From the aspects of ethnicities, Macedonians comprise 64.2% of the population, Albanians 25.2%, Turks 3.9%, Roma 2.7%, Serbs 1.8%, Bosniaks 0.8% Aromanians and Megleno-Romanians 0.5% and others 1.0%.

6. The majority of the Macedonian population are Eastern Orthodox Christians (69.6%). The rest of the population according to their religion includes Islam (28.6%), Catholicism (0.4%), Other Christians (0.7%), none (0.5%), others (0.2%).

7. The Macedonian Orthodox Church, as well as the Islamic Religious Community in Macedonia, the Catholic Church, Evangelical Methodist Church, the Jewish Community and other religious communities and groups are separate from the state and equal before the law. The Macedonian Orthodox Church, as well as the Islamic Religious Community in Macedonia, the Catholic Church, Evangelical Methodist Church, the Jewish Community and other religious communities and groups are free to establish schools and other social and charitable institutions, by way of a procedure regulated by law.

8. The official language in the entire territory of the country and in the international relations of the country is Macedonian language, and Cyrillic is the official alphabet, while Albanian is also in official use at state-level and in the municipalities where THE ethnic Albanian minority is more than 20% of the population. Other minority languages (Turkish, Serbian, Romani, Aromanian) are also used for official purposes in local government.

III. Political System

9. The first Macedonian Constitution was adopted on 31 December 1946. It was founded on the constitutional decisions of the First Session of the Anti-Fascist Assembly of the National Liberation of Macedonia (ASNOM) of 2 August 1944, being a pillar for the contemporary Macedonian state. In the subsequent constitutional development, constitutions were adopted in 1963 and 1974 (providing the right to self-determination of Macedonia as one of the constituent republics of the former federation).

10. The Constitution from 17 November 1991 has introduced new constitutional, political and economic system in the Republic of Macedonia. The Constitution officially established private property and political pluralism, market economy and the rule of law, based on the highest international standards related to human and civil rights and freedoms. According to the Constitution, the country is a parliamentary republic, with the division of powers into: (1) legislative, (2) executive, and (3) judicial.

11. The Assembly/Sobranie is composed of 120 to 140 members/representatives elected for four years. The Representatives are elected at general, direct, and free elections and by secret ballot. They represent the citizens and make decisions in the Assembly in accordance with their personal beliefs. The mandate of the representatives cannot be revoked. The mode and conditions of election of Representatives are regulated by a law adopted by a majority vote of the total number of Representatives. The Assembly: adopts and changes the Constitution; adopts laws and gives the authentic interpretation of laws; determines public taxes and fees; adopts the budget and the balance of payments of the Republic; adopts the spatial plan of the Republic; ratifies international agreements; decides on war and peace; makes decisions concerning any changes in the borders of the Republic; makes decisions on association in and disassociation from any form of union or community with other states; issues notice of a referendum; makes decisions concerning the reserves of the Republic; sets up councils; elects the Government of the Republic of Macedonia; elects judges to the Constitutional Court of the Republic of Macedonia; carries out elections and discharges judges; selects, appoints and dismisses other holders of public and other office determined by the Constitution and law; carries out political monitoring and supervision of the Government and other holders of public office responsible to the Assembly; proclaims amnesties; and performs other activities determined by the Constitution. In carrying out the duties within its sphere of competence, the Assembly adopts decisions, declarations, resolutions, recommendations, and conclusions.

12. The position of the President is mainly formal, while the Government/Vlada has the key role in executive branch. The President is elected for a five-year term and can be re-elected only once more. The President represents the Republic. The President of the Republic is Commander-in-Chief of the Armed Forces. The President of the Republic exercises his/her rights and duties on the basis and within the framework of the Constitution and laws.

13. The Government is composed of a Prime Minister and Ministers. The Prime Minister and the Ministers cannot be Representatives in the Assembly. The Prime Minister and Ministers are granted immunity. The Government decides on their immunity. The Prime Minister, Deputy Prime Ministers and Ministers cannot be called up for duties in the Armed Forces.

14. The Constitutional Court is a body of the Republic protecting constitutionality and legality. The Constitutional Court is composed of nine judges. The Assembly elects the judges to the Constitutional Court by a majority vote of the total number of Representatives. The term of office of the judges is nine years without the right to re-election. The Constitutional Court elects a President from its own ranks for a term of three years without the right to re-election. Judges of the Constitutional Court are elected from the ranks of outstanding members of the legal profession. The Constitutional Court of the Republic of Macedonia: decides on the conformity of laws with the Constitution; decides on the conformity of collective agreements and other regulations with the Constitution and laws; protects the freedoms and rights of the individual and citizen relating to the freedom of conviction, conscience, thought and public expression of thought, political association and activity as well as to the prohibition of discrimination among citizens on the ground of sex, race, religion or national, social or political affiliation; decides on conflicts of competency among holders of legislative, executive and judicial offices; decides on conflicts of competency among Republic bodies and units of local self-government; decides on the answerability of the President of the Republic; decides on the constitutionality of the programmes and statutes of political parties and associations of citizens; and decides on other issues determined by the Constitution.

15. Macedonian legal system belongs to the civil law (Romano-Germanic) legal family. Judiciary power is exercised by courts. Courts are autonomous and independent. Courts judge on the basis of the Constitution and laws and international agreements ratified in accordance with the Constitution. There is one form of organization for the judiciary. The judicial branch includes Basic Courts, Appellate courts and a Supreme Court. The Judicial Council is an independent and autonomous institution of the judiciary. The Council shall ensure and guarantee the independence and the autonomy of the judiciary.

16. The Public Prosecutor's Office is a single and autonomous state body carrying out legal measures against persons who have committed criminal and other offences determined by law; it also performs other duties determined by law. The Public Prosecutor's Office carries out its duties on the basis of and within the framework of the Constitution and law. The public prosecutor is appointed by the Assembly for a term of six years and is discharged by the Assembly.

17. The Ombudsman protects the constitutional and legal rights of citizens when violated by bodies of state administration and by other bodies and organizations with public mandates. The Ombudsman is elected for a term of eight years, with the right to one re-election.

18. The right of citizens to local self-government is guaranteed. Municipalities are units of local self-government. Within municipalities, forms of neighbourhood self-government may be established. Municipalities are financed from their own sources of income determined by law as well as by funds from the Republic. Local self-government is regulated by a law adopted by a two-thirds majority vote of the total number of Representatives.

19. The following major political parties characterize the political system: Internal Macedonian Revolutionary Organization – Democratic Party for Macedonian

National Unity (VMRO-DPMNE), Social Democratic Union of Macedonia (SDSM), Democratic Union for Integration (BDI), Alliance for Albanians (AA), The Left (Levica), Alternative (Alternativa), Liberal Democratic Party (LDP), etc.

20. The country is a member of: Bank for International Settlements (BIS); Central European Initiative (CEI); Council of Europe (CE); Euro-Atlantic Partnership Council (EAPC); European Bank for Reconstruction and Development (EBRD); Food and Agriculture Organization (FAO); International Atomic Energy Agency (IAEA); International Bank for Reconstruction and Development (IBRD); International Civil Aviation Organization (ICAO); International Criminal Court (ICCt); International Criminal Police Organization (Interpol); International Development Association (IDA); International Federation of Red Cross and Red Crescent Societies (IFRCS); International Finance Corporation (IFC); International Fund for Agricultural Development (IFAD); International Labour Organization (ILO); International Maritime Organization (IMO); International Monetary Fund (IMF); International Olympic Committee (IOC); International Organization for Migration (IOM) (observer); International Organization for Standardization (ISO); International Red Cross and Red Crescent Movement (ICRM); International Telecommunication Union (ITU); International Trade Union Confederation (ITUC); Inter-Parliamentary Union (IPU); Multilateral Investment Guarantee Agency (MIGA); North Atlantic Treaty Organization (NATO); Organisation internationale de la Francophonie (OIF); Organization for Security and Cooperation in Europe (OSCE); Organisation for the Prohibition of Chemical Weapons (OPCW); Partnership for Peace (PFP); Permanent Court of Arbitration (PCA); Southeast European Cooperative Initiative (SECI); United Nations (UN); United Nations Conference on Trade and Development (UNCTAD); United Nations Educational, Scientific, and Cultural Organization (UNESCO); United Nations High Commissioner for Refugees (UNHCR); United Nations Industrial Development Organization (UNIDO); United Nations Interim Force in Lebanon (UNIFIL); Universal Postal Union (UPU); World Confederation of Labour (WCL); World Customs Organization (WCO); World Federation of Trade Unions (WFTU); World Health Organization (WHO); World Intellectual Property Organization (WIPO); World Meteorological Organization (WMO); World Tourism Organization (UNWTO); World Trade Organization (WTO); World Veterans Federation.

IV. Population Statistics

21. According to the data from 2002 the Macedonian population has 2,022,547 inhabitants. Skopje, the capital city, has a population of 506,926. The distribution of the population in the other cities is as follows: Bitola – 74,550; Kumanovo – 70,842; Prilep – 66,246; Tetovo – 52,915; Veles – 43,716; Štip – 43,652; Ohrid – 42,033; Gostivar – 35,847; Strumica – 35,311; Kočani – 8,330; Kičevo – 27,067; Struga – 16,559; Radoviš – 16,223; Gevgelija – 15,685; Debar – 14,561; Kriva Palanka – 14,558; Sveti Nikole – 13,746 and Negotino – 13,284.

22. Concerning the age of the population, the following figures are estimated: 0–14 years: 16.16%; 15–24 years: 12.65%; 25–54 years: 44.47%; 55–64 years: 12.55%; 65 years and over: 14.17%. The median age is total: 39 years; male: 38 years; female: 40 years (2020 est.). The urban population represents 59.1% of total population (2022). The literacy rate of the population 15 years and above is 98.4% (*source*: The World Factbook).

§2. Historical Background

23. Several archaeological sites indicate settlements in prehistory. Such are the findings from the Palaeolithic age.[1] Also, numerous several exceptionally important and developed settlements and necropolises from the neolith, aeneolithic, bronze and iron age have also been registered, such as Velushka Tumba, Mogila, Shuplevec, Crnobuki, Karamani and Beranci.[2]

24. As far as antiquity is concerned, the territory of modern Republic of Macedonia mostly encompassed the ancient kingdom of Paeonia, and part of Upper Macedonia, a region which became part of the kingdom of Macedon in the early fourth century BC. The Roman province of Macedonia was created in 148 BC incorporating the former kingdom of Macedon also Epirus, Thessaly, and parts of Illyria and Thrace. After the split of the Roman into eastern and western halves in the fourth century CE, Macedonia became part of the Eastern Roman/Byzantine Empire.

25. Of particular importance for the world legal history in general is the emergence of the historical scene of the Byzantine Emperor Justinian I (482–565), born as Petrus Sabbatius, in Tauresium (nowadays the village of Taor near the capital Skopje), known for his legislation (known as Corpus Iuris Civilis), one of the greatest achievements for the foundation of contemporary legal science, specially in the area of private law.

26. In the early 860s the brother Saints Cyril and Methodius created the first Slavic Glagolitic alphabet. Their cultural heritage was further promoted by their disciples Saint Clement and Saint Naum who have founded the Ohrid Literary School.

27. The Samuil's rule (997–1014) has marked the middle age since it encompassed most of the Balkans. After the fall of its Empire, the Byzantine rule is re-established.

---

1. Šalamanov-Korobar, L., Analysis of Chipped Stone Artifacts from Middle Paleolithic Lazers in the Cave Golema Pešt, Maced. acta archaeol. No. 21 pp. 1–538 Skopje 2019.
2. Naumov, G., Trzeciecki, M., Przybyła, M., Chwiej, M., Bugaj, M., Szczepanik P., Podsiadło, M.: Archaeological, Topographical and Geophysical Research on the Neolithic Tells in Pelagonia, Sprawozdania Archeologiczne 66, 2014.

28. The Ottoman rule in Macedonia began in 1392 after the battle at the Marica River. In the subsequent 520 years, as part of the province or Eyalet of Rumelia. One of the first rebellions was in 1564–1565 when the peasants were organizing the Mariovo-Prilep Rebellion. Other important Uprisings during the Ottoman rule are the Karposh Uprising in the regions of Kriva Palanka and Kumanovo in 1767; Negus Uprising in 1822; Razlovci Uprising in 1876; Kresna Uprising in 1878–1879.

29. The cultural revival in the nineteenth century included struggle by prominent scholars and writers such as: the Miladinovi brothers, Kuznman Shapkarev, Grigor Prlichev, Gjorgji Pulevski and many others.

30. The process of foundation of the Macedonian Revolutionary Organization was initiated in 1893 with the establishment of the revolutionary committee by Hristo Tatarchev, Damjan Gruev, Ivan Hadzhinikolov, Petar Poparsov, Hristo Batandzhiev and Anton Dimitrov. The Ilinden uprising on 2 August 1903 is considered as one of the most important events, due to the proclamation of the Krushevo Republic.

31. The subsequent period marked a high degree of atrocities and suffering, especially during the Balkan wars 1912–1913, the First World War 1914–1918 and the Second World War 1939–1945.

32. On 29 November 1945, the Federal People's Republic of Yugoslavia was proclaimed in which the People's Republic of Macedonia became one of the constituent republics, according to the decisions of the First Session of ASNOM on 2 August 1944.

33. On 8 September 1991, a referendum was held for the sovereignty and independence of the Republic of Macedonia, which adopted a new constitution on 17 November 1991. The Republic of Macedonia became a UN member on 8 April 1993.

Chapter 1. Copyright and Neighbouring Rights

§1. Sources – Legislation

34. In the Republic of North Macedonia, sources of copyright law are the Constitution, the Law on Copyright and Related Rights (CL), as well as other relevant laws, by-laws, and the ratified international treaties. EU law is not a direct source of law as North Macedonia is not yet an EU Member State;[3] however, by virtue of the Stabilization and Association Agreement,[4] as the main legal framework that sets out the relations between North Macedonia and EU in the accession process, there is an obligation to harmonize the national laws with the EU acquis in this area.[5]

35. The Constitution of the Republic of North Macedonia,[6] as the highest-ranking source of law in the national legal order, establishes copyright protection as one of the fundamental human rights and freedoms. Article 47 of the Constitution guarantees the 'freedom of scientific, artistic and other types of creation', and guarantees 'the rights arising from scientific, artistic or other types of intellectual creation'. This article also stipulates that the state shall 'encourage, assist and protect the development of science, arts and culture'.

36. The main source of copyright law is CL. The current Law was adopted in 2010 and was last amended in 2016.[7] It is a systemic instrument covering the entire area of copyright and related rights. The Law incorporates all relevant international treaties and the EU acquis in this area.[8] In addition to the CL, other laws govern certain copyright aspects, including the Law on Customs Measures for Enforcement of Intellectual Property Rights Protection[9] which applies to export or import of infringing goods, the Criminal Code (CrC)[10] which defines copyright criminal offences, the Law on Audiovisual Media Services, the laws in the field of civil procedure and administrative procedure, Law on Obligations, laws governing inspection, etc.

---

3. It is officially a country with a candidate status for EU membership, currently awaiting the start of EU accession negotiations.
4. Stabilization and Association Agreement: https://eur-lex.europa.eu/legal-content/EN/LSU/?uri=CELEX%3A22004A0320%2803%29.
5. For analysis of the copyright legislation in the Republic of Macedonia *see* Kambovska, M. (2010). Avtorskoto pravo vo vo Evropskata unija I vo Republika Makedonija: Predizvici vo Digitalnoto Opkruzuvanje [Copyright Law in the European Union and in the Republic of Macedonia: Challenges in the Digital Environment]. Doctoral Dissertation, Iustinianus Primus Law Faculty Skopje.
6. The Constitution was adopted in 1991, with subsequent thirty-six amendments adopted in the period until 2019.
7. Official Journal of the RNM Nos 115/2010, 140/2010, 51/2011, 147/2013, 154/2015 and 27/2016.
8. At the time of writing of this publication, there is an ongoing process to pass amendments to the Law, in order to transpose EU Directives 2011/77/EU (Term Directive), 2012/28/EU (Orphan Works Directive), 2014/26/EU (CRM Directive), as well as the WIPO Marrakesh Treaty.
9. Official Journal of the RNM Nos 88/2015, 154/2015, 192/2015 and 23/2016.
10. The current Criminal Code was adopted in 1996 and has been amended on numerous occasions in the period until 2018.

37. In addition, by-laws regulate in more detail certain issues established in the Law on Copyright. At present, there is only one Rulebook adopted by the Ministry of Culture in 2011, which prescribes the elements of the application for a collective rights management licence.

38. International treaties ratified by the national Parliament are part of the national legal order. North Macedonia has ratified all relevant treaties, including among others the Berne Convention (WIPO), the Rome Convention (WIPO), the Internet treaties – WCT and WPPT (WIPO), the TRIPS Agreement (WTO), and the Convention on Cybercrime (Council of Europe).[11]

§2. Subject Matter of protection

39. The Macedonian copyright law belongs to the continental legal tradition, meaning that its focus is on the protection of the author. This is reflected in the legal terminology (in Macedonian: avtorsko pravo) which is a close translation of the French concept of droit d'auteur. The scope of protection granted by the CL covers the right of authors in their copyright works (copyright), the rights of performers, phonogram producers, videogram producers (film producers), broadcasting organizations, publishers and database makers in their subject matter of related rights (related rights), the exercise and the protection of copyright and related rights and the application of the Law.

40. The CL is structured in the following titles: general provisions, copyright, neighbouring rights, collective rights management, protection of rights (enforcement), application of the Law, and transitional and final provisions.

I. Different Categories of Protected Works

41. Protected copyright works are defined quite broadly in the Law on Copyright, in Article 12 paragraph 1, as intellectual and individual creations in the field of literature, science and art, expressed in any manner and form. The Law provides a non-exhaustive exemplary list of types of works that enjoy copyright protection, but the assessment whether a work is protected under the Law should always be based on the mentioned definition and not based on the list. The following types of works are listed as protected copyright works in Article 12 paragraph 2:

(1) written work (book, paper, article, handbook, brochure, treatise and other works of the same nature);
(2) computer program, as a written work;
(3) spoken work (lecture, speech, address, and other works of the same nature);
(4) musical work, with or without words;

11. A full list of treaties to which North Macedonia has acceded is available at (28.09.2021) https://wipolex.wipo.int/en/treaties/members/profile/MK.

(5) dramatic work, dramatico-musical work, choreographic work and a work of pantomime;
(6) photographic work and a work created in a process analogous to photography;
(7) audiovisual work (cinematographic work and other work expressed in moving images);
(8) works of fine art (painting, drawing, print, sculpture, etc.);
(9) works of architecture;
(10) works of applied art and design; and
(11) cartographic work, plan, sketch, technical drawing, project, table, plastic work and other work of identical or similar character in the domain of geography, topography, architecture and science.

42. Only two of these types of works are further defined in the CL. The Law contains separate provisions on computer programs, including a definition in Article 95. The Law also has a separate section on audiovisual works (Article 88–94). In Article 88, audiovisual work is defined as a cinematographic or other work expressed in the form of a sequence of moving images, whether or not accompanied by sound, regardless of the type of the carrier which contains it. The section contains provisions on the authorship in the audiovisual work and contract for film production.

II. Works Excluded from Protection

43. Certain categories of creations are not considered as copyright works and are not protected by the CL (Article 16). Those are creations that lack one or more of the elements that define copyright works as specified in Article 12 paragraph 1. The first category includes ideas, theories, concepts, operation methodologies, or mathematical concepts, regardless of the manner of explanation or expression. Official texts of a political, legislative, administrative and judicial nature and their official translations are also not protected. Out of scope of protection are also daily and other news that have the character of mere media information, miscellaneous facts and data. Finally, ideas and concepts which underlie any element of a computer program, including the program components that enable connection and interaction between the elements of the software and of the hardware equipment (interfaces), are not protected under copyright.

III. Special Categories of Works

A. Computer Software

44. Computer programs are considered as copyright works, equated with written works.[12] The Law on Copyright defines a computer program in Article 95 as a

12. *See* Art. 12 para. 2 item 2 quoted above.

program in any electronic form of expression, including the preparatory design material, provided that it is an individual and intellectual creation. The Law contains several provisions specific to computer programs, concerning the rights of the author, limitations on the rights, and decompilation, which closely reflect the EU Directive on Computer Programs 2009/24/EC.[13]

B. Databases

45. According to the CL, a database is a copyright work, and it is defined in Article 15 paragraph 2 as a collection of data, arranged in systematic or methodical way, and individually accessible by electronic or other means. The copyright in the database does not extend to any computer programs used in the making or operation of the database accessible by electronic means.

46. It should be noted that the Law in this segment has been harmonized with the EU Database Directive 96/9/EC.[14] In addition to granting the status of copyright works to databases, the Law also grants a sui generis protection to the makers of databases.

C. Others

47. Other creations that can be considered as copyright works are adaptations, component parts of a work, and collections of works. The adaptation of a copyright work is considered as a copyright work if it fulfils the conditions of the Law (Article 12 paragraph 3). According to Article 13, any component part of the copyright work, as well as the title of the work, insofar as it is intellectual and individual creation by itself, is considered as a separate copyright work. As a consequence, it is not permitted to use as the title of a copyright work a title that is protected by copyright and which has already been used for a work of the same type if that title would create or would lead to confusion regarding the copyright work and the author. Pursuant to Article 14, a collection of copyright works, of expressions of folklore, of data or of other material, which, by reason of the selection and arrangement of its component parts, constitutes an individual and intellectual creation is considered as a copyright work. The provision gives examples of such collective works, including encyclopaedia, anthology, book of papers, music collection, collection of photographs, maps, exhibition, placement, collection of documents, and other collections. This provision makes it clear that the copyright in the collection of works does not extend to its component parts and does not affect the rights in such parts.

---

13. Directive 2009/24/EC of the European Parliament and of the Council of 23 Apr. 2009 on the legal protection of computer programs, available at (29 Sep. 2021) https://eur-lex.europa.eu/legal-content/EN/ALL/?uri=celex:32009L0024.
14. Directive 96/9/EC of the European Parliament and of the Council of 11 Mar. 1996 on the legal protection of databases (amended by Directive 2019/790), available at (29 Sep. 2021) https://eur-lex.europa.eu/legal-content/EN/TXT/?uri=CELEX%3A01996L0009-20190606#M1-1.

§3. Conditions of Protection

I. Formal Requirements

48. As North Macedonia has acceded to the Berne Convention and other copyright treaties, the national legislation does not require any formalities for copyright protection. This principle is explicitly stated in the Copyright Law, in Article 17 paragraph 2, where it is prescribed that the copyright belongs to the author by the mere act of creation of the work. So, any work that fulfils the criteria of being considered as copyright work[15] is automatically protected under the Copyright Law, even if it is not published.

49. This, however, does not prevent the author or the right holder from taking preventive actions for protection, by registering and depositing originals or copies of his work, phonogram, videogram or other subject matter of his right with a notary or a legal representative (Article 179). The purpose of such preventive action is to preserve evidence, for instance, in case the author or right holder needs to prove his authorship in a court of law, but he can choose to do that for other reasons as well. In addition, according to Article 180, the holder of an exclusive copyright may denote the original or the copies of his work or the videogram with the designation © before his name, pseudonym or designation, together with the year of the first publication. Likewise, the holder of an exclusive right in a phonogram may denote the original or the copies of his published phonogram or their containers with the symbol p before his name, pseudonym or designation together with the year of the first publication. As said, these measures are purely optional, intended primarily for evidence purposes, and they do not affect in any way the copyright protection granted under the Law.

II. Substantive Requirements

50. The substantive requirements are in essence the elements contained in Article 12 paragraph 1, which defines the notion of a copyright work as 'an intellectual and individual creation in the field of literature, science and art, expressed in any manner and form'. This definition can be deconstructed into five elements:

(1) There has to be a 'creation' as the subject matter of protection.
(2) Intellectual creation. In order for a work to be protected as copyright work, it has to be an intellectual creation. This requirement is related to the originality concept. It is not further defined, but it is typically considered that an intellectual creation is the result of a thought process elaborated beyond a mere idea into a specific expression of some kind.
(3) Individual creation. This is strongly linked with the concept of authorship and moral rights, which rest on the personal link of the author with her work. As

15. Art. 12 para. 1.

a consequence of this requirement, only works created by one of the more specific individuals can enjoy copyright protection. Legal persons (companies, organizations) cannot be considered as authors, only as right holders following transfer of specific rights from the author.

(4) Creation in the field of literature, science and art. This requirement defines, in a broad way, the areas of creation that can produce copyright works.

(5) Creation expressed in any manner and form. This is a reflection of the fixation requirement. It means that first, the creation needs to be expressed to be protected by copyright; it has to be manifested in some definite perceptible form since it is the expression which is protected and not the idea. This expression of the creation can be fixed in any manner and take any form. Thus, for copyright protection, it is completely irrelevant how the creation is expressed – whether in physical or digital form, whether on paper, on a tree trunk, by singing, by moving, by text, by visuals, etc. This is left to the author's freedom and creativity, as long as the creation is expressed in some manner and form.

§4. Ownership

I. The Author (Initial Authorship)

51. The notion of author is defined in Article 17 of the Copyright Law. The author is a natural person who has created the copyright work, and the copyright belongs to the author by the mere act of creation of the work. The fact that only individuals, natural persons, can be authors is an expression of the underlying foundation of the Macedonian copyright system in the 'author's right' (droit d'auteur) concept. It is reflected in the 'intellectual and individual' nature of the creation as a requirement for copyright protection.

52. As there are no formal requirements for copyright protection, the Law establishes a legal presumption of authorship (Article 18), whereby the person whose name, pseudonym, code or other sign is denoted in a usual manner on the work or its copies, or is indicated at the time of its disclosure, is considered to be the author until proved to the contrary. So, in order to establish the authorship, it is sufficient to have any kind of identifiable designation which can be linked to a particular person or persons.

53. If the author is unknown, nor can he or she be determined based on any identifiable designations, the copyright will be exercised by the person who has lawfully disclosed the copyright work, until the moment the author's identity is established. In that case, the person who exercised the copyright will be obliged to surrender to the author the economic benefits acquired from the exercise of copyright, unless otherwise agreed between them by contract.

54. The CL contains provisions on the scope of application *ratione personae*. The protection granted under the CL can be enjoyed by authors who are citizens or have their principal establishment in the Republic of Macedonia. Foreign authors enjoy the same protection based on international agreements ratified in accordance with the Constitution. Foreign authors who do not enjoy protection under international agreements enjoy protection if one of the following criteria specified in Article 189 is fulfilled:

(1) foreign authors who are domiciled in the Republic of Macedonia;
(2) works that are first published in the Republic of Macedonia or published in the Republic of Macedonia within thirty days from the day of first publication in another country;
(3) audiovisual works whose producer has his principal establishment or domicile in the Republic of Macedonia; and
(4) works of architecture or fine art which, as an immovable property or a component part thereof, are located on the territory of the Republic of Macedonia.

55. If the copyright work has been created by several authors, the protection is enjoyed by all of them if at least one of them meets any of the above conditions.

56. In other cases, foreign authors may enjoy the same protection on the basis of factual reciprocity. The CL specifies that, in any case, foreigners enjoy protection with respect to their moral rights in all cases, and with respect to the right of resale only on the condition of factual reciprocity. The burden of proof of reciprocity is on the person relying on it.

57. According to Article 194, protection under the CL is enjoyed by a foreign author whose work is communicated to the public in the Republic of Macedonia through satellite broadcasting. The protection is enjoyed in any case if an uplink station which transmits the program-carrying signals is situated in the Republic of Macedonia, or if the broadcasting organization that has commissioned the broadcast by satellite has its principal establishment in the Republic of Macedonia.

58. Authors who have no citizenship or whose citizenship cannot be determined – stateless persons – as well as foreign authors having the status of refugees under the national regulations benefit from the principle of national treatment if they have a domicile or a necessary residence in the Republic of Macedonia. The persons who have neither domicile nor necessary residence enjoy the same protection as the citizens of the state in which they have a domicile or necessary residence.

II. Joint Works/Works Created by Several Persons

59. When a work is created in collaboration with two or more persons, the copyright belongs to all those persons who are co-authors (Article 19 paragraph 1). The Copyright Law contains provisions governing the mutual relations between the co-authors further in Article 19. The consent of all the co-authors will be necessary for every use of the joint work, and an individual co-author cannot refuse to give his consent for reasons that are contrary to the principle of conscientiousness and good faith. If the work is composed of independent parts (divisible whole), each co-author can authorize independent use of his part, provided that such use does not prejudice the use of the joint work or the rights of the other co-authors. The share of each co-author in the remuneration from the use of the work will be determined in proportion to the real contribution that each one of them had in the creation of the work, unless otherwise agreed by them. In case where the real contribution cannot be determined, or where no agreement has been reached between the co-authors, each co-author will be entitled to an equal part of the remuneration.

60. The Copyright Law contains separate provisions on authorship in audiovisual works (Articles 89–90). Authors of an audiovisual work are the author of the screenplay, the principal director and the principal cameraman. In case when animation of any kind is an essential element of the work, the principal animator is also considered as author. Where music is an essential element of the work, the author of the music specially created for use in the audiovisual work is also considered as author. The animator and the music author, when not considered as authors of the audiovisual work, as well as the set designer, the costume designer, the editor, and the make-up artist, have copyright only in their own contributions to the audiovisual work, and are considered as authors of contributions.

III. Works Made for Hire

61. There are separate provisions in the Copyright Law on 'copyright work in the course of employment'. Article 86 stipulates that when a copyright work is created by an employee in the course of execution of his duties or following the instructions of the employer, it will be considered that the economic rights of the author have been exclusively transferred to the employer. This transfer is valid for a period of five years from the completion of the work. The article gives the freedom to the author and the employer to agree on different arrangements in a collective agreement or employment contract. After the expiry of the five-year period, the economic rights belong to the employee. In this case, the employer can demand another exclusive transfer provided that he pays the employee remuneration for each separate type of economic right transferred. The Law protects the author by granting him an unwaivable right to remuneration for each rental, regardless of the transfer of his rights to the employer.

62. The following Article 87 provides exceptions from the transfer in the course of employment. The employee retains the exclusive right to use the copyright work created in the course of employment as part of his collected works. The other exception concerns computer programs and databases. Under Article 87, it is considered that the economic rights in computer programs and in databases are transferred to the employer without any limitations, unless otherwise provided by contract.

§5. TRANSFER

63. It should be clarified that, since the Macedonian copyright law is rooted in the continental civil law system, there is no concept of assignment of copyright. The CL speaks of 'transfer' of rights, and there are provisions on certain copyright contracts, which could be broadly likened to licences, but the CL itself does not use the term 'license' either. A separate section of the CL (Articles 63–98) lays out the general rules governing the transfer of rights as well as rules on specific copyright contracts and other special situations like employment and computer programs.

64. In the context of transfer of rights, it is worth mentioning that in some cases, the management of rights, including the granting of licences to users, is carried out by collective management organizations. The CL contains an entire title four devoted to the collective rights management system. As a general principle, under Article 129, holders of copyright and related rights may manage the rights individually (separately for each copyright work or subject matter of a related right), personally or through a representative, or collectively (jointly for several works or subject matters of related rights and for several right holders) through an organization for collective rights management, in a manner and under conditions provided by the CL.

65. Collective rights management covers legal matters with the users of rights, mainly the granting of non-exclusive licences, collection of remunerations from the use and their distribution, and protection of rights before the state authorities and other entities. Collective management can be carried out only for published copyright works and published subject matter of related rights. In the case of collective management, the rights are transferred on a non-exclusive basis.

66. Collective management of copyright and related rights is carried out by an organization for collective management, which is a legal person founded by right holders (natural and legal persons) for collective management that operates on its own behalf and for the account of the right holders, based on a licence from the Ministry of Culture (Article 132).

I. Assignment of Copyright

67. Assignment of copyright, as understood under common law, is not possible under the Macedonian copyright legal system. The national copyright law follows the 'monistic' approach and views the right of the author as one whole. There are explicit provisions in the CL to this effect. Article 20 of the CL is a provision containing the general principles on the contents of copyright. It states that 'the copyright is an indivisible right and it is inseparable from the copyright work' and that the copyright (literal translation would be the 'author's right' which more clearly points to the wholeness of the right and its link with the author) consists of exclusive moral rights, exclusive economic rights and other rights. The transfer of copyright as a whole, through contract or through any other means, is null and void (Article 67 item 1).

68. Further, there are provisions on the relationship between copyright and right of ownership (Articles 6–7) that make it clear that the copyright, as a rule, is an autonomous right and it is independent of the ownership right or other rights in the objects in which the copyright work is incorporated. As a legal consequence of this, the transfer of economic rights of the author of the work does not affect the ownership right in the object where the copyright work is incorporated, and the opposite is also true – the transfer of the ownership right does not affect the transfer of the economic rights of the author of the work.

II. Licences

69. As mentioned, the CL does not use the term 'licenses', but 'transfer' of rights. Section six of the CL contains provisions on the transfer of economic rights (Article 63 et seq.) Only economic rights can be subject to transfer. Concerning moral rights, following the author's death, certain moral rights, namely the right of recognition and right of integrity of the work, can be managed by the successors. The author can transfer to other persons separate economic rights, on an exclusive or non-exclusive basis (scope of transfer) in a manner and under conditions provided by the CL.

70. When it comes to the scope of transfer of an economic right, it can be exclusive or non-exclusive (Article 70). The transfer is exclusive when the author authorizes a single person to use the work, while the author or any other person is excluded from the use. The transfer is non-exclusive when the author authorizes a person to use the work, while the author or any other person is not excluded from the use.

71. There are three ways in which the transfer of economic rights can be carried out:

(1) succession;
(2) written contract (exclusive or non-exclusive);
(3) other written way (non-exclusive) by an authorization, statement, approval, etc.

72. The CL contains only general provisions regarding succession as a legal basis for transfer, in Article 64. It states that economic rights are subject to succession, and that the author's successors acquire all the rights that would have belonged to the author. The details on succession of copyright are governed by the succession regulations.

73. The principal manner of transfer of economic rights is by contract (Article 65). There is a legal requirement that the contract is concluded in a written form; otherwise, it will not produce a legal effect. The Law specifies the mandatory elements of the copyright contract. The contract needs to contain, in particular, the type of the rights being transferred; their scope, exclusive or non-exclusive; the territory concerned by the transfer of rights; the duration of the transfer; and the author's remuneration. There is a provision protecting the author as the weaker negotiating party, according to which any disputed or ambiguous contractual provisions must be interpreted in the author's interest.

74. There is a separate provision on the author's remuneration, as an especially important element of the contract which the legislator deemed appropriate to regulate in more detail (Article 66). The author's remuneration needs to be determined according to the principle of fairness, the type of the work, the type and the scope of the right that is being transferred, the duration, and other relevant circumstances of its use. If the use of the work generates revenue which is significantly larger than the agreed remuneration, the author has the right to demand a revision of the agreed remuneration, which will allow him a more equitable share of the revenue, and the author cannot waive this right. The remuneration revision is a reflection of the principle *rebus sic stantibus* which is well established in the Macedonian contract legislation, specifically the Law on Obligations Relations.[16] In addition, obligations are imposed on the user of the work relating to transparency and provision of information. If the author's remuneration is agreed or determined according to the revenue derived from the use of the work, the user of the work is obliged to keep appropriate books or other records that allow determining the amount of the generated revenue. The user is also obliged to enable the copyright holder to inspect the documentation/records, and to submit to him the necessary reports on the generated revenue within a reasonable time period, unless the time period has been defined by law or by contract.

75. In some situations, the transfer will be null and void (Article 67). This is the case of transfer of the copyright as a whole, the transfer of the moral rights, or the transfer of unknown types of use of the copyright work.

76. Apart from the provisions on transfer contained in the CL as a *lex specialis*, the general regulations governing contracts, primarily the Law on Obligations, apply to contractual transfer of economic rights (Article 68).

77. Active legitimation is defined in Article 69 of the CL. The rights that belong to the author, including the right of judicial protection, also belong to any other right holder, in a scope transferred to him by law or by other legal act.

---

16. Art. 122 on termination or change of the contract due to the change of circumstances, Law on Obligations Relations (Official Journal Nos 8/01, 78/01, 04/02, 59/02, 05/03, 84/08, 81/09, 161/09, 23/13, 123/13, 215/21).

78. Since the CL entitles the author to choose which economic rights to transfer and under what conditions, the CL contains a rule of separate transfer (Article 71), under which the transfer of a particular economic right does not affect the transfer of other economic rights. However, there is a presumption of joint transfer in the case of the right of reproduction. Article 72 stipulates that when transferring the right of reproduction, it is considered that the right of distribution of the copies of the concerned work has also been transferred, unless otherwise provided by contract.

79. The CL regulates subsequent transfer in Article 73. A holder to whom an economic right of the author has been transferred cannot, without the author's authorization, subsequently transfer that right to a third party, unless he is permitted to do so by contract. If the subsequent transfer is the consequence of a legal transformation of the right holder, the authorization from the author is not required. If the subsequent transfer is allowed without the author's authorization, in accordance with law or with contract, the previous and the new holder shall be jointly and severally liable for any claims by the author.

80. Cancellation of the transfer is regulated in Article 74. The author can cancel the contract or withdraw the authorization or another written act for transfer of an economic right if the holder of the exclusive right exploits it to an insufficient extent or does not exercise it at all, thereby significantly harming the author's interests. This right is unwaivable. The author cannot exercise the cancellation or the withdrawal if the reasons for the cancellation are attributable to him. The author can choose to offer to the right holder an additional time period for appropriate use of the right. When the author chooses to exercise the cancellation or the withdrawal, the economic right returns to him. In that case, the author will be obliged to pay adequate compensation for damages to the right holder, if so, required by the principle of fairness.

81. The CL contains a separate section with provisions on certain types of copyright contracts (Articles 75–87) concerning publishing contract, public performance contract, contract for commission of a copyright work, and provisions on transfer in the course of employment (covered above), and there are special provisions on transfer of rights in film production in a subsection relating to audiovisual works (Articles 88–94). With respect to these situations of contractual transfer of rights, the CL is a *lex specialis* that applies in addition to the general rules on contracts contained in other regulations, primarily the Law on Obligations.

(1) Publishing contract

82. The publishing contract, stipulated in Article 75, is a legal act by which the author transfers to the publisher his right of publication, which consists of the right of reproduction of his work and distribution by printing it in a hardcopy form in a sufficient number of copies intended for the public. The publisher is obliged to pay remuneration to the author, publish the work and distribute the published copies.

83. The publication right does not include the right of publication of the work in an electronic form, which requires the conclusion of a separate contract. In this case, the publisher who has the right of publication of the work in a hardcopy form has a right of priority, among equal bidders, for the publication of the work in electronic form. The right of priority runs for three years from the publication of the work in a hardcopy form. The publisher has to respond in writing within thirty days from the receipt of the author's offer. The right to a pocket edition, periodical edition or publication in sequels, translation and alike can be also transferred by the publishing contract.

84. Concerning the contents of the publishing contract (Article 76), the CL stipulates that, in addition to the general elements of copyright contracts, it must include a deadline for submitting the manuscript for the purpose of publication, number of separate editions and number of copies (circulation) for each separate edition. The remuneration in the publishing contract can be determined as a lump sum, or as a percentage of the retail price of a copy of the edition. In case when the remuneration is agreed as a percentage of the retail price of the sold copies of the work, the publisher is obliged to enable the author inspection in the documentation concerning the sold copies.

85. There is a presumption of exclusivity (Article 77) under which it is considered that, during the validity period of the publishing contract, the author has transferred exclusively to the publisher the right of publication of the work in the same language, except for newspaper articles, unless the contract provides otherwise.

86. The publisher is obliged under Article 78, for the subsequent editions, to enable the author to make improvement or alteration to the work, provided this does not cause significant cost for the publisher and does not substantially alter the work, unless otherwise provided by the publishing contract.

87. Article 79 contains provisions on destruction of the work due to force majeure. If the manuscript of the work is destroyed due to force majeure after delivery to the publisher, the author has the right of remuneration that would have been given to him if the work had been published. If an entire prepared edition is destroyed due to force majeure before it has been distributed, the publisher has the right to prepare a new edition, and the author has the right of remuneration for one edition only. In case when part of a prepared edition is destroyed by a force majeure before it has been distributed, the publisher has the right to print only as many copies as were destroyed without payment of additional remuneration to the author.

88. Termination and cancellation of the contract are governed by Article 80. The publishing contract is terminated if the author dies before completion of the copyright work, if the circulation of all agreed editions is sold out, if the term of validity of the contract has expired, and in other cases provided by law or by contract. The author can cancel the publishing contract if the publisher, after the circulation of the previous edition has been sold out, does not publish new agreed editions within the time period stipulated in the publishing contract. In case of cancellation, the author has the right to keep the received remuneration or to demand payment of the agreed remuneration, as well as the right to request compensation for damages. The circulation is considered sold out if the number of unsold copies is less than 5% of all agreed and published editions, and in any case if the number is less than one hundred copies. In case when the publisher intends to destroy the unsold copies of the work, he is first obliged to offer the copies to the author (Article 81).

(2) Public performance contract

89. With the public performance contract, the author transfers to the user the right of public performance of his work (Article 82). Given the definition of public performance in the CL (Article 31), the subject of a public performance contract can be the live performance in the form of speaking or reciting of literary works; performance of musical works and stage performance or live presentation of dramatic, dramatico-musical, choreographic, or pantomime works. In addition to the general elements of copyright contracts, this contract may also include the right of the author of inspection of the public performance of the work, and the duty of the user to allow that to the author and to provide adequate technical conditions for the performance (Article 83). In case when the work has not been performed within the agreed time period or under the agreed conditions, the author has the right to cancel the contract, keep the already received remuneration, demand payment of the agreed remuneration, and request compensation for damages (Article 84).

(3) Contract for commission of a copyright work

90. Contract for commission is one where the author creates the commissioned copyright work and delivers it to the commissioning person (Article 85). The person commissioning the work has the right to supervise the work and give instructions, unless by doing so he encroaches upon the author's freedom of creation. The author retains the copyright in the commissioned work, unless otherwise provided by law or by contract.

(4) Contract for film production

91. The contract for film production (Article 91) regulates the relations between the film producer on the one hand, and the authors of the audiovisual work and the authors of contributions on the other hand, as well as the relations between the authors themselves. The CL established a presumption of exclusive, unlimited transfer of the rights when concluding the film production contract: 'it shall be considered that the authors and the authors of contributions have transferred to the film producer, exclusively and without limitation, all their economic rights in the audiovisual work, including the right of translation by subtitling or dubbing, unless otherwise provided by contract'. The authors keep the right to equitable remuneration from the film producer for every use, and the authors of contributions keep the right to use their contributions to the audiovisual work separately, unless by doing so, they infringe the rights of the film producer. The authors and the authors of contributions may not waive these rights. The film producer is obliged, at least once a year, to deliver to the authors of the audiovisual work a report on the generated revenue, separately for every type of use of the work.

92. The completion of the audiovisual work, as an essential element of the contract, is detailed in Article 92. The audiovisual work is considered completed (created) when the principal director determines that the first standard copy of the work, which is the subject matter of the contract, is completed. Alterations to the first standard copy of the audiovisual work are possible only after prior approval by the principal director and the film producer. In case when one of the authors or authors of contributions does not complete his part of the audiovisual work or is unable to do so due to a force majeure, he may not object to the use of the created part for the completion of the work. The author enjoys appropriate copyright in that part.

93. Cancellation of the contract by the authors is possible in case when the film producer fails to complete the audiovisual work within five years from the conclusion of the film production contract, or where he fails to distribute the completed audiovisual work within one year after its completion, unless another time period has been agreed (Article 93). In the case of cancellation, the authors and authors of contributions retain the right of payment of remuneration.

94. Due to the nature of the transfer of rights by the film production contract (exclusive and without limitations), certain general provisions are not applicable to the film production contract (Article 94). This is the case with the rule on separate transfer of economic rights (Article 71) and the rules on subsequent transfer subject to the author's authorization (Article 73). In addition, the author's moral right of withdrawal is also not applicable (Article 21 paragraph 1 item 4 and Article 25).

§6. Scope of Exclusive Rights

I. Moral Rights

95. Moral rights are those that arise from the intellectual, individual link of the author with her work. Article 21 contains the principle that the moral rights 'protect the author with regard to his personal and spiritual (intellectual) ties to the work'. The CL established four exclusive moral rights of the author, all of which are unwaivable. These are the right to claim authorship (Article 22); right of first disclosure (Article 23); right of protection of the integrity of the work (Article 24); and right of withdrawal (Article 25).

96. The author has the right to claim authorship of the work. What this means is that the author has the right to have his name, pseudonym, or other designation denoted on each copy of the work, or stated at each public use of the work. This means that the duty to indicate the authorship falls on the user of the work. The exception to this is only if the author explicitly declares in a written form that he does not want to have his authorship denoted, or if at the time of the use it is technically impossible or impractical.

97. The right of first disclosure means that only the author has the right of first disclosure of his copyright work and the right to determine the conditions of disclosure. He can freely decide when, how, and under what conditions he can disclose his work for the first time. Until the time of the first disclosure, only the author has the right to publicly reveal the content or the description of his work.

98. The right of protection of the integrity of the work means that the author can object to any modification, distortion, or mutilation of the work, which would be prejudicial to his personality, honour and reputation, as well as to object to the destruction of the work.

99. After an economic right of the author has been transferred, the author retains the right of withdrawal. The author has the right to withdraw the right of use from the right holder, in case where any further use would be prejudicial to his personality, honour, and reputation. If the author withdraws the right of use, he is obliged to compensate the holder for the damage caused by such withdrawal. The right holder needs to inform the author of the amount of damage that needs to be compensated within three months from the receipt of the withdrawal. If he fails to do so, the withdrawal becomes valid upon the expiration of that time period. Upon the withdrawal, the economic right returns to the author. If the author wishes to transfer again the economic right in his work, he is obliged to offer such transfer primarily and under the same conditions to the same right holder. This right does not apply to computer programs, the rights in audiovisual works transferred with a film production contract, and electronic databases.

II. Exploitation Rights

100. The exploitation rights, or economic rights as they are called in the CL, protect the property interests of the author in his copyright work (Article 26). As a general rule applicable to all types of economic rights granted under the CL, the author has the exclusive right to authorize or prohibit the use of his work or copies thereof by any other person, except in the cases provided by the CL. It follows from this general principle that the economic rights are exclusive by nature, meaning the author can freely choose if he wants to authorize (by concluding a contract or otherwise) or prohibit any use of his work, and this also extends to the copies of the work. The exclusivity that the author enjoys with respect to his economic rights is restricted only in the cases defined as exceptions or limitations to the rights in the CL.

101. The CL defines in Article 27 four types of exclusive economic rights of the author that arise from the use of the copyright work or its copies:

(1) right of reproduction of the work;
(2) right of distribution of the work;
(3) right of communication to the public of the work; and
(4) right of adaptation of the work.

102. It should be noted that some of the economic rights are subject to mandatory collective rights management. Pursuant to Article 130 of the CL, collective management is carried out in cases where the management cannot be carried out individually, due to the character of the copyright works or subject matter of related rights and due to the conditions and manner of their use. For exclusive rights that can be managed individually, the authors and right holders can choose to entrust the management to a collective organization with contract. The CL gives the possibility to authors and right holders to opt out from collective rights management with a statement certified by a notary which prohibits the organization from managing his rights.

103. Article 131 specifies the rights that, as a rule, are managed collectively:

(1) communication to the public of non-stage musical works and non-stage literary works;
(2) the author's right of royalty from the right of resale;
(3) the author's right of remuneration for public lending;
(4) the right of remuneration of the author and the performer for rental of phonograms or videograms;
(5) the right of remuneration of the performer for broadcasting and other communication to the public of his performance which in itself is a broadcast or is made from a fixation;
(6) the right of remuneration of the performer and the phonogram producer from the single equitable remuneration for communication to the public of phonograms with performances published for commercial purposes;
(7) the right of fair compensation of the author and the publisher from reproduction on paper or similar carrier by photocopying or any other analogous technique having similar effects, for private use;
(8) the right of fair compensation of the author, the performer and the phonogram producer for the reproduction of the phonogram for private use;
(9) the right of fair compensation of the author, the performer, and the film producer for the reproduction of the videogram for private use; and
(10) the right of cable retransmission of copyright works and subject matter of related rights which, as an exclusive right, is managed collectively on a compulsory basis, except for works and subject matter of related rights that are rebroadcasted by a broadcasting organization, regardless of whether the concerned right is its own or the rebroadcasting right has been transferred to it by another right holder.

104. In practice, there is presently only one functioning collective management organization, ZAMP, which has been in existence for several decades. It manages the authors' music rights, including the right of communication to the public, and the cable retransmission right. The payments are agreed upon agreements concluded with users, or based on the tariff adopted by ZAMP.

A. Reproduction Right

105. Reproduction (Article 28) is defined broadly, as a fixation, i.e., recording of the work in a material or other appropriate medium (electronic and other), as well as making one or more copies of a copyright work, in whole or in part, directly or indirectly, temporarily or permanently, by any means and in any form. The CL gives examples of the ways of making reproductions. It states that the reproduction is carried out, in particular, by graphic processes (graphic reproduction), by three-dimensional reproduction, by photocopying and other photographic processes achieving the same effect, by building or carrying out works of architecture, by sound or visual fixation, by storage of the work in electronic form (electronic fixation), and by transfer of the work from an analogue onto a digital system.

B. Distribution Right

106. The distribution right under the Macedonian CL relates to the physical distribution of copyright works. Distribution is defined in Article 29 as making available to the public an original or a copy of the work, for the purpose of sale or other forms of transfer of ownership right or right of possession, including importation and rental, and covering the right of remuneration for lending. So, rental and lending as particular types of uses are covered under the concept of distribution.

107. Importation, rental and lending are defined as well. Importation means placing on the domestic market originals or copies of a copyright work intended for further circulation for commercial purposes. Rental is making available for use an original or a copy of a copyright work for a limited period of time, for direct or indirect economic advantage. The rental does not apply to constructed works of architecture and originals and copies of works of applied art and design. Lending means making available for use of a copyright work, for a limited period of time, by organizations which are accessible to the public, without obtaining direct or indirect economic advantage.

108. The principle of exhaustion of the right of distribution is implemented in the CL. The right of distribution in the territory of the Republic of Macedonia is exhausted with the first sale or other forms of first transfer of ownership right of an original or copy of a copyright work, carried out by the right holder or with his consent. The exhaustion does not apply to the rights of importation, rental and lending.

C. Performing Right

109. The CL, being part of the continental legal system, contains the concept 'communication to the public' rather than performing/public performance. The right of communication to the public is defined as a separate exclusive right in Article 30. It is a broad right encompassing seven types of use defined in Articles 31–37:

(1) Public performance. Public performance can be live speaking or reciting of works in the field of literature; live performance of musical works; or stage performance or live presentation of dramatic, dramatico-musical, choreographic, or pantomime works.
(2) Public transmission. Public transmission means communication to the public by loudspeaker, screen or by any other technical means, of live performance of a copyright work, outside of the space or place where the work is performed live; audio and/or visually fixed works (phonograms, videograms, etc.), from the medium in which they are fixed; or a broadcast copyright work.
(3) Public exhibition. Public exhibition is presentation to the public of an original or a copy of a work of fine art, a work of photography or a work created in a process analogous to photography, a work of applied art, design, architecture, physical planning, cartography, as well as other works of scientific and technical nature.
(4) Public presentation. Public presentation is presentation to the public, by technical means, of an audiovisual work or of a work of photography, fine art, architecture, physical planning, applied art, design, cartography, and works of scientific and technical nature.
(5) Broadcasting. Broadcasting is defined as communication of a copyright work by radio and television program signals intended for reception by the public, either wireless, including satellite, or by wire, including cable, microwave, or other systems. Satellite is any satellite operating on frequency bands which, according to the telecommunications regulations, are reserved for the broadcast of signals intended for the reception by the public or which are reserved for closed, point-to-point communication, in which case the conditions for the signal reception must be comparable to the conditions for the reception by the public. Broadcasting by satellite is carried out when, under the control and responsibility of the broadcasting organization, program-carrying signals intended for the public are introduced into an uninterrupted communication chain leading to the satellite and down towards the earth. If the program-carrying signals are encrypted, the broadcasting by satellite is considered as carried out if the decrypting means are provided to the public by the broadcasting organization or by some other person, with the consent of the organization.
(6) Rebroadcast. Rebroadcast is simultaneous, unabridged and unaltered transmission of a broadcast of a copyright work, provided that it is carried out by a broadcasting organization other than the one which initially broadcasted the work (rebroadcasting); or it is carried out by a cable, or microwave, system, where the initial broadcast is carried out by a broadcasting organization wireless or by wire (cable retransmission).
(7) Making available to the public. Making available to the public is communication to the public of a copyright work, by wire or wireless means, including Internet or other communication networks, in a way which allows members of the public to access the work, from a place and at a time individually chosen by them.

D. *Adaptation Right*

110. Article 38 defines the concept of adaptation as a translation, modification, including audiovisual adaptation, musical arrangement or other alteration of a copyright work or of an expression of folklore, as well as of other written materials, such as translations of official texts which are not made for official use. The rights in the copyright work created with the adaptation do not affect in any way the rights in the adapted work. As translation is considered as a form of adaptation, the CL does not contain a separate translation right.

E. *Other Rights*

111. In addition to the exclusive moral and economic rights, the CL contains a separate section on other rights of the author. These are rights that are granted due to the specific nature of the works – works of art, rights of remuneration for lending and rental, and right of fair compensation for private copying which is an exception permitted by the CL. The other rights that the author enjoys under the CL are listed in Article 39:

(1) right of access and delivery;
(2) right of resale (right of royalty from resale);
(3) right of fair compensation for reproduction for private use;
(4) right of remuneration for lending; and
(5) right of remuneration for rental.

1. Right of Access and Delivery

112. Article 40 lays out the rights and duties in case of access and delivery of a copyright work in possession of a party other than the author. The author has the right to access the original or the copy of his work in possession by another person, for the purpose of exercising the right of reproduction or adaptation of the work, insofar as it does not conflict with the legitimate interest of the possessor. The author can demand from the possessor to deliver to him the original of the work of fine art or of the photographic work for the purpose of public exhibition or other form of disclosure if there is justified interest. The delivery of the original may be subjected to lodging of an appropriate security or to insurance in the amount of the market value of the original. The author is obliged to carry out the access and delivery with the least possible inconveniences to the possessor, and at his own expense. In case of damage to the work, the author is liable regardless of his fault.

2. *Droit de suite* (Right of Resale)

113. The right of resale of an original work of art is governed by Articles 41–45 of the CL. The general principle is that the author has the right to be notified and to obtain royalty from every subsequent sale or other disposals of an original of a work of art. The rationale behind this right is that, due to the nature of works of art as original and unique objects, their commercial value often increases with time. The resale right cannot be subject to waive, disposal or judicial execution.

114. The CL defines the material scope of application of this right by providing a definition of an original work of art in the context of the right of resale. An original work of art to which the right of resale is applicable means a work of fine art, graphic art or plastic art, such as: paintings, collages, drawings, prints, engravings, lithographs, sculptures, ceramics, carvings, tapestries, glassware, photographs or works created in a process analogous to photography, as well as copies of the mentioned works that are considered as originals. Copies of the mentioned works created by the author himself or made with his authorization in limited numbers, like a series of prints, are considered as originals. They need to be, in a usual manner, numbered, signed or otherwise duly indicated by the author.

115. The CL prescribes the rates for determining the author's royalty from the resale right:

(1) 5% for the portion of the sale price from 300 up to 3,000 EUR;
(2) 4% for the portion of the sale price from 3,000.01 up to 50,000 EUR;
(3) 3% for the portion of the sale price from 50,000.01 up to 200,000 EUR;
(4) 1% for the portion of the sale price from 200,000.01 up to 350,000 EUR;
(5) 0.5% for the portion of the sale price from 350,000.01 to 500,000 EUR;
(6) 0.25% for the portion of the sale price exceeding 500,000 EUR.

116. There is a cap on the maximum amount of the royalty that the author can receive, which is set at 12,500 EUR.

117. The CL determines the parties obliged to pay the royalty. The author's royalty is jointly payable by the seller of artworks, the art dealer, the organizer of the auction, or the other intermediary who carries out the sale of artworks.

118. The royalties are calculated in MKD counter value according to the standard exchange rate of the National Bank of the Republic of Macedonia on the day of the sale. The basis for calculating the royalties is the sale price, excluding the value added tax (VAT).

119. A separate provision (Article 44) governs the right of resale of a manuscript. If the original (the manuscript) of a literary or musical work has been sold or otherwise disposed of, its author has the right to be notified of every subsequent resale and to obtain for each one a royalty in the net amount of 3% of each sale price. The cap, the parties obliged to pay, and the manner of calculation apply *mutatis mutandis* to the resale of manuscripts as well.

120. In addition to the right to receive royalty, the author enjoys the right to information. This right entitles the author, his successors or the societies for collective management of copyright, within three years from the day of the sale of the copyright work, to request from the parties obliged to make payment any information that may be necessary to secure payment of the royalty from the resale, in particular concerning the titles of the sold works, the owner and the intermediary, the sale contracts and the sale price.

121. The right of royalty from resale is subject to mandatory collective management. As there is no organization established yet to manage this right, the provisions of the CL relating to the resale right are not implemented, and the royalties are not collected in practice.

3. Right of Fair Compensation for Reproduction for Private Use

122. The reproduction for private purpose is allowed as an exception in the CL, as a type of use for which no authorization of the author is needed; however, it is subject to payment of fair compensation. The author has the right to a part of the fair compensation for the reproduction of phonograms and videograms and for the photocopying of his work, which is carried out for private use. This right may not be subject to waive, disposal or judicial execution.

123. The fair compensation for reproduction of phonograms and videograms is paid at the time of the first sale or import of equipment for sound and visual fixation and new blank sound or sound and image carriers. The fair compensation for photocopying is paid at the time of the first sale or import of photocopying equipment, and upon making photocopies intended for sale, on a monthly basis, according to the possible number of photocopies. In order to make this right technology-neutral, the CL specifies that the equipment for sound and visual fixation is considered equal to all other devices which enable to achieve the same effect, and the photocopying is equalized with other reproduction techniques.

124. The duty to pay fair compensation rests with producers and importers of equipment for sound and visual fixation, photocopying equipment, blank sound or sound and image carriers, as well as persons providing photocopying services. These parties are obliged, upon request by the relevant organization for collective management of copyright and related rights, to submit data concerning the type and number of sold or imported equipment and sound or sound and image carriers, as well as data concerning photocopies made.

125. The amount of fair compensation is determined by a by-law adopted by the Government. The fair compensation should be determined separately for each type of equipment for audio and visual fixation, for each fixation equipment which, due to its construction, does not require any special material to function (in an amount twice as much as the usual), for each sound or sound and image carrier based on the recording time, for each photocopying equipment based on the possible number of copies per minute and based on the possibility to copy in colour (in an amount twice as much as the amount for black and white photocopying), as well as for each photocopy intended for sale. The Government should harmonize the amounts of the compensations according to the fluctuation of the prices and the costs of living in the country.

126. Due to the mass nature of private copying, the right of fair compensation for private copying is subject to mandatory collective management. However, to date, no organization has been established to manage this right and collect and distribute revenues to right holders. The Government has not adopted the by-law that needs to specify the details of the fair compensation. So, the right holders do not yet receive revenues on the basis of this right.

4. Right of Remuneration for Rental

127. This right is applicable to authors of music works and authors of audiovisual works. The author who has transferred his right of rental to the phonogram producer or to the film producer retains the right of remuneration for every rental of his work. The author may not waive this right.

5. Right of Remuneration for Lending

128. The author has an unwaivable right of remuneration for the lending of an original or copy of his copyright work. The lending right does not apply to architectural structures, works of applied art and design, or works that are mutually lent by public institutions in the field of science, culture and education (libraries, film archives, scientific and educational institutions). The remuneration is payable by the organization which is carrying out the lending. However, the public institutions mentioned above are exempted from the duty of payment of the remuneration.

6. Others

129. There are special provisions on the rights of authors of computer programs, modelled after the EU Computer Programs Directive as a result of the specificity of computer programs and the ways in which they are used.

130. Under Article 96 of the CL, the author of the computer program has the exclusive economic right to use the program and to authorize or prohibit the use of the program for:

(1) reproduction, as well as loading, displaying, running, transmission or storage of the computer program, insofar as these acts necessitate such reproduction;
(2) translation, arrangement or any other adaptation, as well as reproduction of the results thereof, without prejudice to the rights of the person who made that adaptation; and
(3) distribution as well as lending of the original or the copies of the computer program in any form.

§7. Limitations or Exemptions to the Scope of Copyright Protection

131. The limitations and exceptions in the CL are in line with the EU acquis and the international treaties. Following the continental copyright legal tradition, they are listed in a separate section of the Law (Articles 51–54), except for the limitations to the rights in computer programs which are provided in the section relating to computer programs. There are also separate provisions on the limitations on the rights of database makers.

132. Exceptions and limitations relate to situations where a work is used without authorization, and this use can be against payment, or it can be free, without payment to the author or other right holder. As a general rule, a copyright work can be used without authorization by the author, with or without remuneration, only if the work has been disclosed. The CL implements the three-step test, as a general principle that applies to any type of use permitted without authorization. According to the CL, the use can be carried out only in certain special cases, provided that the use does not conflict with the normal exploitation of the work, and does not unreasonably prejudice the legitimate interests of the author.

133. Article 52 contains an exhaustive list of exceptions that are classified as 'use without payment of remuneration'. Many of these relate to some public interest, and there is a specific non-commercial purpose requirement. The type of use is in some cases specified (reproduction, communication to the public), but in other cases, any 'use' of the work can qualify as exception provided it meets the prescribed criteria. The use of a copyright work without payment of remuneration applies to the following cases:

(1) Temporary reproduction of a copyright work, provided the reproduction is of transient or incidental character, and/or it constitutes an integral and essential part of a technological process, provided the reproduction does not, in itself, have an independent economic significance and the sole purpose of which is to enable the transmission of data in a network between third parties by an intermediary or to enable lawful use of the work.
(2) Reproduction made by public libraries, educational establishments or museums, or by archives, for the purpose of carrying out their activity and without direct or indirect economic or commercial purpose.

(3) Fixation of a copyright work by a broadcasting organization that has an authorization to broadcast the work, if it fixes the work by means of its own facilities and for its own needs, and provided it destroys the fixation within the period for which the broadcasting authorization is valid. If the fixation has exceptional documentary value, it can be delivered and preserved in a public archive.

(4) Use of works for illustration for teaching or scientific research to the extent justified by the non-commercial purpose to be achieved, provided that the name of the author and the source are indicated, unless this turns out to be impossible.

(5) Use of copyright works for the benefit of persons with special needs in a way which is directly related to the special need, to the extent required by the need and for a non-commercial purpose.

(6) Reproduction and public communication of texts, articles and other similar works concerning current economic, political, religious and other similar topics, with the aim to inform the public, to the extent justified by that purpose, unless it is expressly prohibited by the author and provided that the name of the author and the source are indicated, unless this turns out to be impossible.

(7) Use of parts of copyright works (quotations), for scientific research, education, criticism, polemics, or review, in a scope and to the extent required by the specific purpose and provided that the name of the author and the source are indicated, unless this turns out to be impossible.

(8) Use of works for the purposes of public security, or in a judicial, parliamentary or administrative procedure.

(9) Use of political speeches, as well as extracts of public lectures and similar works to the extent justified by the informatory purpose, provided that the name of the author and the source are indicated, unless this turns out to be impossible.

(10) Use of works during religious rituals or other official celebrations organized by the state authorities or the local self-government.

(11) Use of architectural or sculptural works permanently located in public places (streets, squares, parks, etc.).

(12) Use of works in the field of fine and applied art, architecture, industrial design and photographic works exhibited at public exhibitions or at auctions, by the organizer, for posters or catalogues made with no commercial purposes, to the extent necessary for promotion of those events.

(13) Adaptation of a work into a parody, caricature, or pastiche, provided that the adaptation does not create confusion with regard to the original of the work and the authorship, and provided the adaptation is in the frames of authorized use of the work.

(14) Reproduction of a copyright work onto a sound and image carrier, public communication of the work from that carrier, as well as public communication of the work that is broadcast, in shops, at fairs and other places where the operation of equipment for recording, reproduction and communication of sound and image is demonstrated, to the extent necessary to demonstrate the functioning of the equipment. The fixations/recordings made on this basis shall be erased immediately.

(15) Incidental (secondary) inclusion of a copyright work into some other material.
(16) Use of drawings or plans of an architectural object, for the purpose of its reconstruction.
(17) Communication to the public and making available to the public of a copyright work for the purpose of research or private study in certain locations within the public scientific, cultural, educational and other establishments of similar nature, in case where a work is not subject to purchase, or its use is not subject to having an authorization, and where the work is contained in the collections/fund of these establishments.

134. There is a separate provision on databases. The use of a database or of a copy thereof by the lawful user is without remuneration if it is necessary for the purposes of access and normal use of its component parts.

135. The use of expressions of folklore is governed in Article 53. Expressions of folklore can be used without remuneration, in a decent manner, without distortion and provided that the source and the origin of the work are indicated. The public and scientific institution Folklore Institute 'Marko Cepenkov' in Skopje is responsible for the management of the use.

136. Article 54 covers use against payment of fair compensation. The use of a copyright work against payment of fair compensation applies to two cases, both relating to reproduction. The first is reproduction on paper or any similar medium, by way of photocopying or any other analogous technique or other process having similar effects, with the exception of graphic editions of a musical work (sheet music). The second is reproduction on any medium, made by a natural person for private use, without direct or indirect commercial purpose (private copying).

137. When it comes to computer programs, there are special provisions on the limitation to the rights (Articles 97–98) for the benefit of the lawful user of the program, allowed without authorization by the right holder. Unless otherwise provided by contract, the lawful user of the computer program can make reproduction, or translation, arrangement or any other adaptation as well as reproduction of the results thereof, including for error correction, when they are necessary for the use of the computer program in accordance with its intended purpose.

138. The lawful user can also make a backup copy when it is necessary for its use. The user may observe, study, or test the functioning of the program in order to determine the ideas and principles which underlie any element of the program, if it is necessary while loading, displaying, running, transmitting or storing the program. These two limitations cannot be overridden by contract.

139. The decompilation is covered in a separate Article 98. The reproduction of the code and translation of its form do not require authorization from the right holder if they are indispensable in order to obtain the information necessary to achieve the interoperability of an independently created computer program with other programs, provided that the following conditions are met:

(1) such acts are performed by a licensee, by another lawful user, or by a person authorized by them, acting on their behalf and for the same purpose;
(2) the information necessary to achieve interoperability has not previously been available to these persons; and
(3) such acts are confined only to those parts of the original program which are necessary to achieve interoperability.

140. The information obtained through the decompilation may not be used for goals other than to achieve interoperability. It may not be given to third parties, except when it is necessary to achieve the interoperability of the independently created computer program. And it may not be used for the development, production or marketing of a computer program that is substantially similar in its expression, or used for any other act which infringes copyright.

141. The provisions concerning decompilation are subject to the three-step test. They may not be applied in a manner which might unreasonably prejudice the copyright or which would be in conflict with the normal exploitation of the computer program.

142. There is a special provision on the limitation on the rights of the database maker (the sui generis right), for the benefit of a lawful user. Under Article 122, the use of the substantial part of the contents of the database by the lawful user is permitted without authorization of the right holder and without remuneration, in the case of:

(1) reproduction from a non-electronic database for private purposes;
(2) reproduction for teaching illustration purposes or for scientific research, as long as the source is indicated and to the extent justified by the non-commercial purpose; and/or
(3) distribution, making available to the public, or other forms of communication to the public, for purposes of public security, in administrative or in judicial procedures.

§8. Duration of Protection

143. The duration of copyright and the duration of related rights are specified in separate sections. The duration of copyright is governed by Articles 55–62 of the CL. There are different terms of protection for economic rights and for moral rights.

144. The economic rights run for the life of the author and for seventy years after his death. In cases of co-authorship, the term of duration of economic rights is calculated from the death of the last surviving author. In the case of co-authorship of an audiovisual work, the term of protection is calculated from the death of the last surviving person from among the following: the principal director, the author of the screenplay, the author of the dialogues and the composer of the music created especially for use in the audiovisual work, regardless of whether that person is recognized as the author of the audiovisual work according to the CL. Copyright of anonymous and pseudonymous works runs for seventy years after the lawful disclosure of the work. If the pseudonym leaves no doubt as to the identity of the author, or if the author reveals his identity during the period of seventy years following the disclosure, the general rule for protection applies – during the author's life and seventy years after his death.

145. For non-disclosed works, the copyright runs for seventy years after their creation. If the term is calculated according to the lawful disclosure of the work, and the work is disclosed in volumes, parts, instalments, issues, episodes and alike, the term is calculated separately for each component part.

146. The terms of copyright protection begin to run on 1 January of the year following the event which is the basis for the calculation of the terms. The copyright work, after the expiration of the terms of duration of the economic rights, can be used without authorization and without remuneration.

147. With respect to moral rights, various terms of duration apply. The moral right of withdrawal runs for the life of the author. The moral rights of recognition and indication of the authorship, and of protection of the integrity of the copyright work, continue to run after the expiration of the terms of duration of the economic rights; in other words, they run indefinitely. For these moral rights, after the author's death, in addition to the author's successors, the relevant professional association of authors, the persons having legitimate interest, and the Macedonian Academy of Sciences and Arts are responsible for their management and protection.

148. The duration of related rights is governed by Articles 123–128. For the performers, the economic rights run for fifty years from the day of the performance. If within this period the fixation of the performance has been lawfully published or lawfully communicated to the public for the first time, the rights of the performer run for fifty years from the first lawful publication or communication to the public. The moral rights of performers continue to run after the expiry of the terms of duration of economic rights. The provision on the management of the author's moral rights of authorship and protection of integrity of the work following his death accordingly applies to the rights of performers.

149. The rights of the phonogram producer run for fifty years from the day of the first fixation of the phonogram. If within this period the phonogram has been lawfully published for the first time, the rights of the producer run for fifty years from the publication. If the phonogram was not lawfully published within this period, and if it has been lawfully communicated to the public, the rights of the producer run for fifty years from the communication to the public.

150. The rights of the film producer run for fifty years from the day of completion of the fixation. If, during that period, the fixation has been lawfully published or communicated to the public for the first time, the rights of the producer run for fifty years from the first lawful publication or communication to the public.

151. The rights of broadcasting organizations run for fifty years from the day of the first broadcast of the program. The rights of the publisher run for fifty years from the lawful publication.

152. The rights in special cases of publishing – when a legal or natural person for the first time lawfully publishes or in other way discloses a copyright work in which the author's economic rights have expired, or when a natural person for the first time lawfully publishes a scientific or a critical commentary or review of a previously published copyright work in which the author's economic rights have expired – run for twenty-five years from the first lawful publication or disclosure.

153. The rights of the maker of the database run for fifteen years after the completion of the database. If within this period the database is lawfully disclosed, the rights run for fifteen years after the disclosure. The term of protection of fifteen years following completion begins to run anew following any substantial change, evaluated qualitatively and/or quantitatively, to the contents of the database, including any substantial change resulting from the accumulation of successive additions, deletions or alterations, which would result in the database being considered to be a substantial new investment, evaluated qualitatively or quantitatively.

154. There is a provision on comparison of terms of duration, in Article 193. Within the scope of application of international obligations, the terms of duration of rights according to the CL apply to foreign holders of copyright and related rights who enjoy protection under the CL, and expire no later than the date of expiry of the protection granted in the country of which they are citizens or in which they have a principal establishment, but in any case, no longer than the terms of duration provided by the CL.

§9. Neighbouring Rights

155. Neighbouring rights (related rights) in the Macedonian CL grant protection to the following categories of subject matter and right holders: performances of performers; phonograms of phonogram producers; videograms of film producers; programs of broadcasting organizations; publications of publishers and databases of database makers.

156. Certain provisions on copyright apply *mutatis mutandis* to neighbouring rights as well. Those are the provisions relating to: relationship between copyright and ownership right (Articles 6–9 and Article 11), component parts and titles of a copyright work (Article 13), presumption of authorship and co-authorship (Articles

18 and 19), definitions of economic rights (Articles 28–38), right of exhaustion following the first sale (Article 29 paragraph 5), exceptions and limitations on the economic rights (Articles 51–54), manner of calculation of the terms of duration and effects from their expiry (Articles 60 and 62), and transfer (Articles 63–71 and Articles 73–74).

157. When it comes to the conditions under which neighbouring right holders are granted protection under the CL, the same provisions as for authors apply (*see* Article 188). Protection is granted to right holders who are citizens or have their principal establishment in the Republic of Macedonia, to foreign right holders based on ratified international agreements, based on connecting factors specific to different types of right holders,[17] or on the basis of factual reciprocity. Foreigners enjoy protection with respect to their moral rights in all cases, and with respect to databases protected with related rights only on the condition of factual reciprocity.

158. The principle of national treatment incorporated in Article 195 applies to related right holders in some situations. Related right holders who have no citizenship or whose citizenship cannot be determined (stateless persons) and those having the status of refugees under the national regulations enjoy the same protection under the CL as the citizens of the Republic of Macedonia if they have a domicile or necessary residence in the Republic of Macedonia. Right holders who have neither domicile nor necessary residence in the Republic of Macedonia enjoy the same protection as the citizens of the state in which they have a domicile or necessary residence.

159. In the case of communication to the public by satellite, according to Article 194, protection under the CL is granted to a foreign holder of related rights whose performance or subject matter of a related right is communicated to the public in the Republic of North Macedonia through satellite. This protection is enjoyed in any case if an uplink station which transmits the program-carrying signals is situated in North Macedonia, or the broadcasting organization that has commissioned the broadcast by satellite has its principal establishment in North Macedonia.

(1) Rights of performers (Articles 101–108)

160. The notion of performers is defined in Article 101. Performers are actors, singers, musicians, ballet dancers and other persons who by acting, singing, dancing, declaiming, reciting, or in some other way perform works of literature and art or expressions of folklore. Directors of stage works, orchestra and choir conductors, sound or sound fixation editors are also considered as performers.

161. Performers who collectively participate in the same performance, such as orchestra, choir, dancing or drama ensemble, group, or other types of collective entity, are obliged to authorize one of the members-performers of the ensemble as

17. These are elaborated below in the respective sections on each right holder.

their representative for transfer of rights of use of the performance, unless otherwise provided by law or by the rules of the ensemble. The authorization must be given in written form and is valid if it is granted by the majority of the performers in the ensemble. The authorization contains the rights for which authorization is given, the total number of performers, their names, signatures of the members granting the authorization, and duration of its validity. These provisions on representatives do not apply to directors of stage works, conductors and soloists.

162. Performers, due to their individual and creative contribution to the performance, have moral rights similar to those of the author. Performers have the following exclusive moral rights to:

(1) be recognized as the performer of the performance;
(2) have his name, pseudonym, or other designation, or the name of the ensemble, the artistic director of the ensemble and the soloist, indicated for every use of the performance, unless it is technically impossible;
(3) object to any alteration, distortion, mutilation or destruction of his performance, and to object to any use of the performance that could be prejudicial to his personality, honour and reputation.

163. A performer has exclusive economic rights to authorize or prohibit the use of his performance for the following uses:

(1) fixation of his unfixed performance;
(2) communication to the public of his unfixed performance, except for broadcasting of a performance which is itself already a broadcast performance or is made from a fixation;
(3) reproduction of the fixation of the performance, meaning making of copies of the fixation;
(4) distribution of the original or copy of the fixation of the performance;
(5) making the fixation of the performance available to the public.

164. In addition to the exclusive moral and economic rights, performers enjoy certain remuneration rights which are unwaivable. The performer has the right to a portion of the single equitable remuneration for every communication to the public of a phonogram containing his performance, published for commercial purpose – meaning reproduction of a phonogram in a sufficient number of copies intended for the public. The performer who has transferred his right of reproduction of the fixation with his performance to a phonogram producer or to a film producer retains the right of remuneration for every rental. Last, the performer has the right to a portion of the fair compensation for reproduction for private use.

165. The performer may transfer to another person his economic rights of use of his performance with a performing contract. The performing contract has to be concluded in a written form and contain, in addition to the general elements provided in the CL, the title of the performed work and the name of the author of the work, as well as the number and period of broadcasts in case where the contract concerns broadcasting.

166. The CL provides for a presumption of transfer in the case of phonogram or film production. Under Article 107, it will be considered that with the conclusion of a contract for the production of a phonogram or audiovisual work, the performer has transferred to the phonogram producer or the film producer all his economic rights, including the right of dubbing of his performance. The CL leaves the possibility to agree differently in the contract.

167. The provisions from Article 86 concerning works created in the course of employment accordingly apply to performances in the course of employment.

168. Foreign performers enjoy protection under the CL, based on Article 190, in cases of performers:

(1) who have a domicile in the Republic of North Macedonia;
(2) whose performances take place in the territory of the Republic of North Macedonia;
(3) whose performances have been fixed on phonograms that enjoy protection under the CL; and
(4) whose performances have been incorporated in broadcasting by radio, but without intention of being fixed on phonograms, that enjoy protection under the CL.

169. If several performers take part in the performance, the protection is enjoyed by all of them, if at least one of them is a citizen of the Republic of North Macedonia or has a domicile in the Republic of North Macedonia.

(2) Rights of phonogram producers (Articles 109–114)

170. Phonogram producers are defined as a natural or legal person who undertakes the initiative, the organization, the financing and the responsibility for the first fixation of sounds of a performance, of other sounds or sound effects. The CL goes on to define phonogram and fixation. A phonogram is the fixation of sounds of a performance, or of other sounds or sound effects, other than fixation contained in an audiovisual work. A fixation is the embodiment of sounds or sound effects into a sound carrier from which they can be perceived, reproduced or communicated with the assistance of technical devices.

171. Concerning the contents of rights, the phonogram producer has the right, for every use of the phonogram, to have his name or designation appropriately indicated, unless it turns out to be impossible. The phonogram producer has the exclusive economic right to use, authorize or prohibit the use of the phonogram for reproduction, distribution, and making available to the public.

172. The phonogram producer has certain other rights, which are remuneration rights. The phonogram producer has the right to a portion of the single equitable remuneration for the communication to the public of his phonogram published for commercial purposes. Phonograms made available to the public are considered as phonograms published for commercial purposes. The phonogram producer and the performer of the performance fixed in the phonogram have the right to an equal share of the single equitable remuneration, unless otherwise provided by contract. The user is obliged for every use to pay the remuneration for the rights of the phonogram producer and for the rights of the performer. In addition, the phonogram producer is entitled to a portion of the fair compensation for reproduction for private use. Under Article 191 of the CL, protection under the CL is granted to foreign phonogram producers whose phonogram has been first fixed in the Republic of North Macedonia.

(3) Rights of the film producer (Articles 112–114)

173. A film producer is defined as a natural or legal person which undertakes the initiative, the organization, the financing, and the responsibility for the creation of the first fixation of an audiovisual work (videogram). The videogram is the image carrier containing the fixation of moving images, with or without accompanying sound, from which they can be perceived, reproduced or communicated with the assistance of technical devices.

174. The film producer has the right to have his name or designation appropriately indicated every time the videogram is used, unless it is impossible. The film producer has an exclusive economic right to authorize or prohibit the use of his videogram for:

(1) reproduction;
(2) distribution;
(3) public presentation;
(4) broadcasting;
(5) rebroadcasting; and
(6) making available to the public.

175. The film producer also has the right to a portion of the fair compensation for reproduction for private use.

176. Pursuant to Article 191, protection under the CL is granted to foreign film producers whose videogram has been first fixed in the Republic of North Macedonia.

(4) Rights of broadcasting organizations

177. Under Article 115 of the CL, a broadcasting organization has exclusive economic rights to authorize or prohibit the use of its programs for:

(1) fixation of the programs into sound and/or image carriers;
(2) reproduction and distribution of the copies of fixations of programs;
(3) rebroadcast;
(4) public transmission, in places accessible to the public against payment of an entrance fee;
(5) making available to the public.

178. Foreign broadcasting organizations enjoy protection under the CL, according to Article 192, if they transmit their programs or broadcasting services through transmitters located on the territory of the Republic of North Macedonia.

(5) Rights of publishers

179. The publisher, defined as a legal or natural person who lawfully publishes a copyright work in a hardcopy form, has the right (Article 116) to a portion of the fair compensation for reproduction for private use.

180. There are also two special cases of publishing which give rise to certain rights to the publishers, regulated in Article 117. The first is when a legal or natural person for the first time lawfully publishes or in other way discloses a copyright work in which the author's economic rights have expired. The second is when a natural person for the first time lawfully publishes a scientific or a critical commentary or review of a previously published copyright work in which the author's economic rights have expired. In both cases, the publisher has exclusive economic rights equivalent to the economic rights of the author.

181. Pursuant to Article 191, protection under the CL is granted to foreign publishers, with regard to their related rights, if the edition has been first published in the Republic of North Macedonia or has been published in the Republic of North Macedonia within thirty days from the day of first publication in another country.

(6) Rights of a database maker (Articles 118–122)

182. The maker of a database is a legal or natural person who undertakes the initiative and responsibility for investing into the creation of a database if he can demonstrate that he has carried out a qualitative and/or quantitative substantial investment in the obtaining, verification or presentation of its contents.

183. The database maker has exclusive right to authorize or prohibit the reproduction (extraction) and/or distribution of copies, making available to the public, or other forms of communication to the public of the whole or of a substantial part of the database (reutilization). The principle of exhaustion applies here as well – the first sale of a copy of a database by the right holder or with his consent will exhaust the right to control further resale of the copy. The rights of the database maker apply without prejudice to the existing rights in the parts incorporated into the database.

184. The protection of the rights of the database maker covers:

(1) the entire contents of the database;
(2) the substantial part of its contents, assessed qualitatively and/or quantitatively;
(3) the insubstantial parts of its contents, when used in repeated and systematic acts which conflict with the normal exploitation or which unreasonably prejudice the legitimate interests of the database maker.

185. The protection of the database does not apply to computer programs used for the making or operation of databases accessible through electronic means.

186. The CL specifies the rights and obligations of the lawful user of the database. The maker of a disclosed database may not prevent the lawful user of the entire database or of a part where he is authorized to use only a part, from using the insubstantial parts of its contents, evaluated qualitatively and/or quantitatively, for any purpose. The lawful user of a disclosed database may not perform acts which conflict with the normal exploitation and/or acts which unreasonably prejudice the interests of the maker of the database. The lawful user of a disclosed database may not cause prejudice to the holder of copyright or related right with respect to works or subject matter of related rights contained in the database. There is a provision on the limitation of the rights, outlining the uses allowed without authorization of the database maker and without remuneration.[18]

§10. Infringement and Remedies

187. The CL contains a separate chapter with provisions on the rights protection and specific enforcement measures (Articles 159–187). Under the Macedonian legal system, copyright and related rights enjoy criminal, civil and misdemeanour protection.

188. The criminal protection is regulated by the provisions of the CrC and the regulations on criminal procedure. The CrC contains several articles that define copyright criminal offences and the corresponding sanctions of imprisonment or fines. These are Article 157 on violation of copyright and related rights, 157-a on violation of the right of the distributor of the technically encrypted satellite signal, 157-b on piracy of audiovisual works, and 157-v on piracy of phonograms.

189. The CL contains provisions relating to civil and misdemeanour protection of copyright and related rights. In addition, civil protection is governed by the regulations on litigation procedure, securing claims, and obligations relations. And the regulations on misdemeanours apply to the misdemeanour protection of copyright and related rights.

190. The protection of copyright and related rights includes the protection of technological measures against rights infringement. The regulations on the customs

18. *See* the section on exemptions and limitations.

measures for protection of intellectual property rights apply to the provisional measures in cases of import, export or re-export of a copyright work, a subject matter of a related right, or a copy thereof.

191. The CL specifies the persons entitled to protection and the types of claims they can submit. A person whose right determined under the CL has been infringed, or there is reasonable doubt that the right will be infringed, and when there is a real threat of a right infringement, is entitled to submit:

(1) request for protection of the right; and
(2) request for provisional and other measures.

192. The procedure based on these requests is urgent.

193. In addition to the author, other persons entitled to protection are the right holder, the person authorized to use the right and the organization. All of them are categorized as 'right holders' in the provisions relating to rights protection.

194. The principle of solidarity of the parties, both on the side of the right holders and on the side of infringing parties, is incorporated in the CL. When a right has been infringed, any of the several holders of that right may demand protection of the right against a third party, as if he is the only holder. When the person who infringed the right fulfils the claims of any of the holders of the same right, his obligation will cease for the rest of the right holders. In case of an ongoing court procedure, the holders of a particular right are considered as a single party. In case of several infringers of a right, each of them is jointly and severally liable for the infringement.

195. In case of protection of a right that is managed collectively, when the organization proves that an infringement has been committed, it will not be necessary for the infringement to be established by the individual holder whose right is managed collectively.

I. Protection of TPMs and electronic management information

196. The CL contains several provisions on the protection of technological measures. It defines technological measures as any technology, computer program, device or their component parts, which in their normal course of operation are designed to prevent or restrict acts of infringement of the rights provided by the CL which are not authorized by the right holder. These measures are deemed effective if the right holder implements them by applying access control or protection process, such as encryption, scrambling or other types of transformation of the work, as well as by mechanisms for copy control.

197. It is considered infringement of an exclusive right if the person knew or could have known that he undertakes any activities for the purpose of circumvention of the effective technological measures for protection of that right. Further, it is considered as infringement of the exclusive rights when a person manufactures, imports for the purpose of distribution, distributes, sells, rents, advertises for sale or rental, or possesses for commercial purposes a technology, computer program, device or their components, or provides services without authorization, of any effective technological measures, which:

(1) are promoted, advertised or marketed for the purpose of circumvention of technological measures;
(2) have only limited commercial purpose or use, other than to circumvent;
(3) are primarily designed, produced, adapted or performed for the purpose of enabling or facilitating the circumvention of technological measures.

198. These provisions accordingly apply to any technology, computer program, device or their components used for removal or alteration of electronic rights management information.

199. There are certain exceptions to the application of technological protection measures. The right holder who uses technological measures is obliged, without delay, and in the shortest period possible, upon request from the person who has lawful access to the copyright work, in case of the exceptions and limitations under Article 52 paragraph 1 items 2, 3, 4, 5 and 8 and Article 54 of the CL, to enable him access and use of the work through removal of the technological measures or through provision of other appropriate means. This rule cannot be overridden by contract. The conditions of the three-step test accordingly apply to these exceptions and limitations. The exceptions and limitations do not apply to the right of making available to the public.

200. Electronic rights management information is similarly protected. Electronic rights management information is any information provided by the right holders which allows identifying the copyright works or subject matter of related rights, including databases, the author, any other right holder, terms and conditions of their use, as well as their appropriate numbers or codes that represent such information. It is considered that a person is infringing the exclusive economic rights when he knowingly, without authorization, removes or alters any electronic information for the rights management, or if he reproduces, distributes, imports for the purpose of distribution, rents, or communicates to the public a copyright work or subject matter of related rights from which electronic rights management information has been removed or altered without authorization, and he knew or could have known that by doing so he is inducing, enabling, facilitating or concealing an infringement of the rights.

II. Civil Actions for Rights Protection

201. The right of protection entitles the right holder to the following claims in a civil procedure:

(1) Termination of the infringement action. The claimant may request from the defendant to cease the infringing action, and/or prohibition of such or similar action in the future.
(2) Compensation of material damages. If material damages have been caused by an infringement of a right, the person has the right to request compensation for the material damages and compensation of lost profits. The compensation is determined in the amount that the defendant would have paid if he had requested to use the right lawfully (usual remuneration), or in an amount stipulated in the relevant tariffs of the collective management organization or in a general agreement.
(3) Compensation of non-material damages. In case of infringement of a moral right, regardless of whether a civil penalty is granted, and in the absence of material damage, the court may award the author payment of an equitable pecuniary compensation for the suffered emotional pain and suffering as a consequence of the infringement of his moral right, if it finds that the circumstances of the case, and especially the degree of the infringement and its duration, have caused that.
(4) Civil penalty. If a right has been infringed intentionally or through gross negligence, the entitled person may request payment of the agreed or the usual remuneration for such type of use, increased for up to 200%, regardless of whether he has suffered material damage as a result of the infringement. When deciding on the request for payment of the penalty and when determining the amount, the court takes into account all the circumstances of the case, and in particular the degree of fault of the defendant, and the amount of agreed or usual remuneration.
(5) Indication of the author. In case of infringement of the moral right concerning the indication of the name, pseudonym or other designation of the author when using his work, the court may decide to have their additional or correct indication.
(6) Return of the benefits acquired from unauthorized use, in accordance with the regulations on obligations.
(7) Removal from circulation of the objects that infringe the right. In case of infringement of an exclusive right, without prejudice to the claims for compensation of damages and regardless of any awarded compensation, the entitled person has the right to request removal from circulation of the copies of a copyright work and subject matter of related rights made without authorization for the purpose of distribution or when they are in distribution, as well as of the materials and equipment used or intended to carry out the infringement, and their destruction. These measures are taken at the expense of the person who has infringed the rights. When pronouncing this measure, the court takes into consideration the circumstances of the case, and in particular the proportionality between the seriousness of the infringement and the claims, the

interest of the person for effective protection of rights, as well as the interests of third parties. The provisions concerning destruction of architectural works apply only where a specially justified reason exists. Where the measures do not correspond to the nature and intensity of the infringement, which may be remedied in some other way, and if the court considers that the person who has committed the infringement has acted unintentionally or without negligence, the court may award to the entitled person, provided he agrees with that, payment of a pecuniary compensation in an amount which cannot be less than the one which he would have obtained from the authorized use of the right. The destruction measures do not apply if the destruction of the equipment used or intended for infringement of a right would cause greater damage than the damage caused by the infringement of the right, except in case of equipment exclusively or primarily intended for infringement. The claims against third parties are limited to three years from the moment the person became aware of the unauthorized production of the objects, or from their distribution or the intention to distribute them, but no later than five years from their unauthorized production or distribution.

(8) Publication of the court judgment. The entitled person has the right to request publication of the final judgment that entirely or partially adopts his claims for protection of copyright and related rights in the mass communication media, at the expense of the defendant.

III. Provisional Measures for Rights Protection

202. If the entitled person submits a request for provisional or other measures, according to the regulations on securing a claim (proposal or legal action) and makes it probable that the copyright is infringed or there is a threat of infringement, the court may issue a provisional measure for cease or prevention of the infringement, by ordering:

(1) prevention of the imminent infringement of the right;
(2) provisional prohibition of right infringement or making such infringement subject to payment of a pecuniary compensation in the amount of the prescribed fine for such type of right infringement, or subject to the lodging of guarantees to ensure the compensation for such type of use;
(3) seizure or prevention of circulation of a copy which is suspected to infringe the right, so as to prevent its import and distribution for commercial purposes;
(4) other similar measures in accordance with the law.

203. The court may issue these measures against an intermediary whose services are used for the right infringement.

204. In case of a right infringement for the purpose of obtaining commercial benefit, and provided that the claimant makes it probable that the right infringement threatens to cause him irreparable harm, the court may order a measure for provisional seizure of the movable or immovable property, as well as the blocking of the bank accounts and other assets of the infringer. To that end, the court may order the communication of bank and financial documents and access to information. The court is obliged to ensure the secrecy of those data, as well as to prohibit their abuse.

205. When a request for provisional measures is submitted, the court may order measures for preserving evidence in particular concerning:

(1) making a detailed description of a copy suspected to infringe the right;
(2) seizure of a copy suspected to infringe the right;
(3) seizure of materials and equipment used in the production and distribution of a copy suspected to infringe the right, as well as any related documents.

206. The provisional measures and the measures for preserving evidence may be ordered without hearing of the opposite party, if the person requesting them shows reasonable evidence that he, or the person who has granted him the power of proxy, is the right holder, and evidence that the right is infringed or there is a threat of infringement, or if any delay is likely to cause irreparable harm to the right holder. If the measure was ordered without hearing of the opposite party, the court submits to it the decision on the measure immediately after its execution.

207. The court needs to specify the duration of the measure in the decision. If the measure is ordered before filing a legal action, the decision contains a time period within which the person requesting the measure is obliged to file a legal action in order to justify the ordered measure, but no longer than twenty working days, counted from the day of delivery of the decision to the person proposing the measure. The procedures for issuing these measures are subject to application of the regulations on securing claims.

208. If a party to the litigation procedure invokes specific evidence and claims that such evidence is held by the opposite party or is under its control, the court will call the opposite party to submit that evidence, determining a time period for the action.

209. In case where the right holder, as a plaintiff, claims in the legal action that a right infringement occurred for gaining a commercial advantage, as well as where he relies in the procedure on banking, financial and similar commercial documents, papers and similar evidence, and claims that they are held by the opposite party or are under its control, the court will call that party to submit the evidence, determining a time period for the action. In these situations, the court decision may not be subject to a special appeal.

210. When a party called to submit evidence denies that the evidence is held by it or under its control, the court may take evidence in order to establish the facts. With respect to the right of the party to refuse the provision of the requested evidence, the right to refuse to testify according to the regulations on civil litigation procedure will apply. The court will judge the significance of the failure by the party to act upon the court decision to submit evidence.

IV. Other Measures

211. The person who has initiated a civil litigation procedure for the protection of rights may request the provision of information on the origin and distribution networks of the work/copy of the work that are used for the infringement of his right. The request may be submitted in the form of a legal action or a provisional measure against a person who:

(1) is sued in a litigation procedure;
(2) in the course of his commercial activity possesses a work/copy of a work suspected to infringe the right;
(3) in the course of his commercial activity provides services suspected to infringe the right or provides services used in an activity suspected to infringe the right;
(4) is indicated as a person involved in the production or distribution of a work/copy of a work or in provision of services suspected to infringe the right, and at the same time is one of the persons indicated in the previous three cases.

212. The request may be submitted as the first claim in a legal action consisting of several claims if the person against whom the request is submitted is sued in the main legal action. The contents of the request include, in particular, information concerning:

(1) names and addresses of the producers and distributors, suppliers and other previous holders of the goods or providers of services, as well as the intended wholesale and retail sellers;
(2) the quantity of produced, manufactured, delivered, received or ordered works/copies of works, as well as their prices.

213. The person against whom the request for provision of information is submitted may refuse to provide such information for the same reasons for which, according to the rules of the Law on litigation procedure, he may refuse to testify. In case where he refuses the provision of information without justified reason, he is liable for damages in accordance with the provisions from the Law on obligations.

214. These provisions do not affect the regulations on the use of confidential information in civil, misdemeanour or criminal proceedings, the regulations governing liability for misuse of the right to obtain information, or the regulations governing the processing and protection of personal data. They do not prevent the application of the provisions on provisional measures and on measures for preserving evidence.

215. In order to preserve evidence or for other reasons, the author or the right holder may, as a preventive action, register and deposit originals or copies of his work, phonogram, videogram or other subject matter of his right with a notary or a legal representative. In addition, right holders can use symbols and designations to denote their work or subject matter of related rights. The holder of an exclusive copyright may denote the original or the copies of his work or the videogram with the designation © before his name, pseudonym or designation, and the year of the first disclosure. The holder of an exclusive right in a phonogram may denote the original or the copies of his published phonogram or their containers with the symbol p before his name, pseudonym or designation and the year of the first disclosure. Unless the contrary has been proved, it is considered that the exclusive rights in the works or phonograms belong to the person indicated according to these provisions. These provisions do not affect or prevent the management and protection of the rights.

V. Misdemeanour Sanctions

216. The CL specifies sanctions for certain misdemeanours in the form of fines, which are imposed on legal persons, on sole traders as well as on natural persons. The specific misdemeanours, the type of sanction and range of fines are set out in Articles 182–187 of the CL.

§11. Overlapping and Relation to Other Intellectual Property Laws

217. From the point of view of legislative and institutional framework, the field of copyright and neighbouring rights is separated from industrial property rights. Copyright falls under the Ministry of Culture, which in its organizational structure contains the Department of Copyright and Related Rights. The Ministry of Culture is the governmental body responsible for the policy and legislative drafting in this field, and for supervision to some extent.

218. With respect to the substance, copyright and industrial property rights are considered as the two segments of intellectual property as a broader theoretical concept. There is some overlapping with industrial design. The CL protects works of applied art and design, without going into further details to describe what those works are, while industrial design according to the Law on industrial property (LIP) protects the design of a product, industrial or handcrafted, which is new and of individual nature. At least, in theory, it is possible that an applied art object can enjoy a double protection as a copyright work and as industrial design.

Chapter 2. Patents

§1. Sources – Legislation

219. Patents are governed by the Constitution, the LIP as well as other relevant laws, by-laws, and the ratified international treaties. Article 47 of the Constitution guarantees the 'freedom of scientific, artistic and other types of creation', and guarantees 'the rights arising from scientific, artistic or other types of intellectual creation'.

220. The main source of patent law is the LIP. Patents are regulated in a separate section of the Law (Articles 25–126). The current Law was adopted in 2009 and was last amended in 2020,[19] with a scope covering all industrial property rights. The Law incorporates relevant international treaties and the EU acquis on patents. In addition to the LIP, other laws govern certain aspects, including the Law on Customs Measures for Enforcement of Intellectual Property Rights Protection[20] which applies to export or import of infringing goods, the CrC[21] which defines criminal offences, the laws in the field of civil procedure and administrative procedure, laws governing inspection, etc.

221. By-laws regulate in more detail certain issues established in the Law. The most relevant is the Rulebook on Patents.[22] Other relevant by-laws govern patents for confidential inventions in the field of defence and security, tariffs for patent registration, rules for obtaining the licence to register IP rights, as well as procedural rules of general application.

222. International treaties ratified by the national Parliament are part of the national legal order. North Macedonia has ratified all relevant treaties, including among others the Paris Convention, the Patent Cooperation Treaty (PCT), and the European Patent Convention (EPC).

§2. Patentable Subject Matter

223. Patent is defined as an industrial property right protecting the invention in procedure before the Industrial Property Protection Office (Office) pursuant to the LIP (Article 3 item 2). The patentable subject matter is defined both in a positive manner, through specifying which inventions are patentable, and in a negative manner by specifying what does not qualify as invention at all. There are exceptions applying to inventions that in principle fulfil the conditions of patentability, but which cannot be patented for ethical or public interest reasons.

19. Official Journal of the RNM nos 21/09, 24/11, 12/14, 41/14, 152/15, 53/16, 83/18, 31/20.
20. Official Journal of the RNM nos 88/2015, 154/2015, 192/2015 and 23/2016.
21. The current Criminal Code was adopted in 1996 and has been amended on numerous occasions in the period until 2018.
22. Official Journal of the RNM Nos 92/2009.

224. Patentable inventions are defined in Article 25 of the LIP. As a general principle, a patent protects an invention in all fields of technology, if it is new, if it contains inventive step and if it can be subject to industrial application. If these requirements are fulfilled, a patent also protects an invention that relates to a product comprising of or containing biological material, or a method for obtaining biological material, for processing it or for using it.

225. The same Article 25 provides a negative definition of what is not considered as a patentable invention:

- a discovery, scientific theory and mathematic method;
- aesthetic creations;
- a plan, rule and a procedure for carrying out intellectual activities, for games, or for carrying out business activity, as well as computer program;
- presentation of information; and
- the human body in different stages of its formation and development or simple discovery of one of its elements, including a sequence or a partial sequence of a gene.

226. An exception to this is possible only if the patent application does not relate to any of these subjects in isolation. In a separate provision, it is specified that an element isolated from the human body or produced by means of a technical process containing a sequence or a partial sequence of a gene may be protected by a patent when the structure of that element is identical to one of the natural elements, whereby the industrial applicability must be contained in the description of invention included in the application form.

227. Article 26 specifies exceptions to patentability. These exceptions relate to inventions that, even though may fulfil the conditions for patentability, cannot be patented. The first is an invention which relates to new animal types and plant varieties and clear biological procedures for creating animals and plants, with the exception of biotechnological inventions, for which the technical feasibility is not restricted to a certain type, and microbiological processes and products generated from such processes. The second is an invention for surgical and diagnostic procedure or treatment procedure of an alive human or animal body, except for an invention that relates to a product, especially a matter or a compound for application of one of these procedures. The final exception relates to an invention the application of which is contrary to the public order or moral, where the application cannot be perceived as such solely because it is forbidden by law. This concerns especially the inventions relating to: cloning processes and modification of human genetic identity of the inheritance line, the use of human embryos for industrial and commercial purposes, the processes of modification of the genetic identity of animals that would most probably cause suffering without providing any significant medical use for the human or the animal, and animals resulting from those processes.

§3. Conditions of Patentability

228. The conditions of patentability, according to the Macedonian LIP, are novelty, inventive step, and industrial application. The first condition, novelty, is regulated in Articles 27–28 of the LIP. The invention is new if it is not covered with the state of the art. State of the art is defined as availability to the world public, by describing the invention in writing or verbally, by using it, or otherwise, prior to the date of filing the patent application, in a manner allowing the expert in the relevant field to apply it. The state of the art also includes the following:

- the contents of the national patent applications, as filed in the Office, except for the patent applications that are rejected, withdrawn, or for which the procedure of examination has been terminated;
- European patents for which protection on the territory of the Republic of Macedonia is requested as recognized and published by the European Patent Organisation (EPO), in compliance with the EPC and the Extension Agreement; and
- international applications, filed in accordance with the PCT, submitted to the Office as elected institution.

229. The provisions relating to the state of the art do not result in an exception from patentability of any substance or compound covered by the state of the art if they should be used in a surgical and diagnostic procedure or treatment procedure of an alive human or animal body as referred to in Article 26 if such use is not contained in the state of the art.

230. When assessing whether the filed invention is new or not, the fact that the invention has become available to the public prior to the expiry of six months after the date of filing of the application does not prejudice the assessment of novelty in the following two cases:

(1) apparent misuse against the applicant or its legal predecessor; or
(2) displaying the invention at official or officially recognized exhibition by the applicant or its legal predecessor in compliance with the Convention on International Exhibitions. This provision applies only if the applicant, when filing the application, invokes the fact that the invention has been exhibited, and submits evidence in writing issued by an authorized institution of the country where it has been exhibited.

231. The second condition of patentability, inventive step, is regulated in Article 29. The invention represents an inventive step if, for the expert in the field, the subject of the invention is not apparently arising from the state of the art as defined in Article 27 of the Law.

232. Last, pursuant to Article 30, an invention is considered susceptible to industrial application if it can be made or used in any kind of industry, including agriculture.

§4. Formalities (Procedure for Grant and Obtaining Patent Protection)

233. According to the LIP, the patent granting procedure can be initiated by the inventor and his legal successor (Article 31). If the invention is a product of the joint work of more inventors, then all the inventors or their legal successors have the right to initiate a patent granting procedure.

234. Under Article 34, the patent granting procedure is initiated by filing the patent application to the Office. The procedure may also be initiated by filing an application in compliance with the PCT, the Extension Agreement and the EPC. Article 35 governs the unity of the invention. It specifies that a separate patent application needs to be filed for each invention. However, one patent application may include multiple inventions when they are interconnected in a way that they make a single inventive concept. There is a separate section with provisions regarding patent applications filed in accordance with international treaties (Articles 116–126).

235. The right of priority is regulated in Articles 36–42. As a rule, from the date of the receipt of a duly filed patent application form in the Office, the patent applicant has a right of priority against any other person that will later file an application for the same invention. The exception to this is when the requirements for recognition of exhibition and union priority right are fulfilled. The person who had exhibited an invention at an officially recognized exhibition or fair of international character in the Republic of Macedonia or in any other Member State of the Paris Union, or the WTO, may submit an application for a right of priority from the first day of exhibition or form the date of use, within ninety days after the date of closing the exhibition (fair). The application form must be accompanied by a certificate by the competent authority of the Member State of the Paris Union or the WTO that the exhibition (fair) is officially recognized in terms of the Convention on International Exhibitions, including data on the type of exhibition or fair, venue, date of opening and closing or date of use. Recognizing the right of priority does not extend the time limits arising from a union priority right.

236. Union priority right is granted in the Republic of Macedonia to the legal or natural person that has duly filed a patent application in one of the Member States of the Paris Union or the WTO, from the date of filing the first application, if so, requested within twelve months from the date of filing the first application. A duly filed application is any application the filing date of which is determined in compliance with the national legislation of the Member State of the Paris Union or of the WTO where it has been filed, or in compliance with international agreements signed between the Member States of the Paris Union. The patent applicant intending to use the union priority right is obliged in the application filed in the Republic of Macedonia to include all the data related to the application he invokes, and within a period of ninety days from the date of filing the application to submit a document on the priority, verified by the competent authority of the Member State of the Paris Union or the WTO, where the first application has been filed.

237. The patent applicant may invoke a multiple priority right on the basis of several previously submitted applications in one or several Member States of the Paris Union or the WTO. If the applicant invokes the multiple priority right, the time limits start running from the date of the recognized priority right, counting from the earliest date of the multiple priority right.

238. The request to recognize a priority right covers only those application elements contained in the first application or applications, on the basis of which the applicant invokes the priority right. If the patent claim, stated in the first application, does not include some of the characteristics of the invention for which the priority right has been requested, it shall be sufficient for the recognition of the priority right if the rest of the elements of the application disclose in detail these characteristics.

239. The Office, at the request of the applicant, will issue a certificate for priority right valid from the date of filing the patent application.

240. The elements of the patent application are specified in Article 43. Mandatory elements of the application are the following:

(1) request for grant of patent. The request must contain a clear indication that grant of patent is requested, the invention title reflecting the essence of the invention, and data on the applicant and the inventor. A written statement in case the inventor does not want to be stated in the application must be filed to the Office within sixty days from the date of filing the application.
(2) description of invention, which should be clear and precise, so that an expert in a certain field is able to apply it.
(3) one or more patent claims. The claims specify the subject matter for which the protection is requested. They need to be clear and included in the description of the invention. The claims can be independent, when they include new, important features of the invention, or dependent, when they include specific features determined by an independent or another dependent patent claim.
(4) abstract concerning the essence of the invention, which is a short summary of the essence of the invention with the sole purpose of providing technical information about the invention. The abstract may not be used for the purpose of defining the scope of the requested protection.
(5) drawing (if needed) to which the description and the patent claim refers;
(6) evidence for paid fee for filing; and
(7) translation into Macedonian language if the application was filed in a foreign language.

241. Other constituent elements and documents are attached to the application.

242. The Office sets the filing date for the patent application if on that day the application includes the following elements:

(1) clear indication that grant of patent has been requested;

(2) data on the applicant, the name and the place of residence or head office; and
(3) part that may be considered as a description of the invention.

243. This does not apply to applications regulated differently by international agreements or the LIP.

244. For the purpose of setting out the filing date, the foreign legal or natural person may file the application and undertake all the actions related to setting out the filing date without an agent if they indicate an address for communication in the Republic of Macedonia.

245. If the application does not have the prescribed contents, the Office will notify the applicant that his application is incomplete and the filing date cannot be set. The Office will invite the applicant, within sixty days upon receipt of the invitation, to correct the shortcomings in the application. If the applicant corrects the application, the Office will set out the filing date of the application. If the applicant fails to eliminate the shortcomings, the application will be deemed withdrawn and the procedure will be closed.

246. Once the filing date of the patent application has been determined, the application may not be additionally altered by extending the subject for which protection is requested. The patent application is entered in a register of patent applications.

247. Since, according to the LIP, the examination procedure can be a full substantive examination or a partial examination by the Office, the applicant should state in the request for grant of patent whether the procedure of examination will be carried out as a full substantive examination[23] or as an examination carried out in the Office. If the applicant fails to indicate the type of procedure, he is obliged to make a statement within twelve months after the filing date.

248. The applicant may divide the subject of the patent application the filing date of which has been determined (the original application) into two or more applications and proceed with a separate procedure on the basis of each of them. The division of the patent application is allowed until a decision for grant of patent is made. The patent application arising from the division of the original patent application (divisional application) keeps the filing date of the original application and the priority of the original patent application.

I. Formal Examination of the Application

249. Pursuant to Article 54, after the patent application has been entered into the register of patent applications, the Office is obliged to check if:

23. The bodies that can carry out full examination are regulated in Art. 63 para 1 item 1 and 2.

(1) the fee has been paid;
(2) a translation into Macedonian language of the application has been submitted, when the application is drafted in a foreign language;
(3) the patent applicant has stated his opinion on the manner of conducting the procedure of examination;
(4) the drawings have been submitted; and
(5) a power of attorney has been attached, when the application had been filed by an agent.

250. If the patent application does not contain these components, the Office invites the applicant within a period no longer than sixty days, from the date of receiving the invitation, to correct the shortcomings. The time limit may be extended for sixty days based on a justified request by the applicant. If the applicant fails to correct the shortcomings, the Office will reject the application.

251. Where the application refers to drawings that are not included in the application, the Office shall invite the applicant to submit the drawings within the specified period. If the applicant fails to proceed, the drawings shall be considered non-existent when examining the application.

252. If the applicant corrects the application within the prescribed period, the application shall be considered as duly filed.

253. In case of a dispute regarding the application right, the applicant may request that the Office considers the application immediately (Article 55). Such request cannot be submitted prior to the expiry of twelve months from the date of filing the patent application. The applicant of the patent application must provide evidence that a substantive examination has been carried out in one of the institutions referred to in Article 63.

II. Procedure for Examination of the Application by the Office (Articles 56–60)

254. Under Article 56, when examining the patent application, the Office shall check whether:

(1) the inventor has been indicated;
(2) priority right recognition has been requested in accordance with the LIP;
(3) the application is in conformity with the invention unity rule stipulated in Article 35;
(4) the elements of the application comply with Articles 43, 44, 45, 46, and 47; and
(5) the subject of the application is an invention, which may prima facie be protected by a patent in accordance with Article 25 paragraph (3), Article 26, Article 27 paragraph (3), and Article 30.

255. The Office shall not examine whether the inventive step requirement has been fulfilled.

256. The Office shall notify the applicant in writing if after the examination it has been established that the requirements under points 1–4 above are not fulfilled, and it shall invite the applicant to correct the shortcomings within sixty days from the receipt of the notification. The Office may extend the time limit for a maximum of sixty days on the basis of a justified request by the applicant. If the applicant fails to correct the shortcomings, the Office shall reject the patent application.

257. The Office shall reject the patent application if the application relates to an invention that may not be protected by a patent within the meaning of item 5 above.

258. The Office may not take a decision to reject the patent application if it did not previously inform the applicant, in writing, about the reasons due to which the requested right cannot be recognized, and if it did not invite the applicant to respond to those reasons within a reasonable time limit. The time limit may be extended to six months on the basis of a justified request of the applicant.

259. If the Office finds that the requirements and conditions stipulated in Article 56 have been fulfilled, it shall notify and invite the applicant within thirty days to pay the costs for patent publication in the journal of the Office, the costs for issuing a patent certificate and the fee for validity maintenance. If the applicant fails to make the payment, the Office shall reject the application.

260. If the requirements from Article 56 are fulfilled and if the applicant pays the costs and fees within the specified time period, the Office shall take a decision for grant of patent. The data from the decision for grant of patent are entered in the Patent Register on the date of the decision and are published in the official journal of the Office within ninety days from the date of the decision.

III. Procedure for Examination of the Application on the Basis of a Substantive Examination (Articles 61–66)

261. When the applicant requests the procedure for substantive examination,[24] the provisions regarding formal examination,[25] request for immediate consideration,[26] and the conditions from Article 56 points 1–4 will apply to the applications.

262. The patent applicant is obliged to submit a request for substantive examination in one of the examining institutions[27] within two years from the date of submitting the patent application to the Office. The applicant needs to submit a copy of

24. Art. 52 para. 1 items 1 and 2.
25. Art. 54.
26. Art. 55.
27. As specified in Art. 63.

the submitted request to the Office. The applicant is obliged, within six months from the date when he received the evidence of the examination referred to in Article 64, to submit to the Office the evidence and translation of the evidence in Macedonian language. If the patent applicant fails to meet any of these requirements, the Office shall decide to reject the application. The Office may not take such decision if it had not previously notified in writing the applicant about the reasons for which it rejected the application and if it failed to invite the applicant within a reasonable time limit to respond. The applicant or the holder of the exclusive right is obliged to present the evidence from the substantive examination also in case of third-party lawsuits due to infringement of the patent right. In this case, the Office shall issue one of the decisions referred to in Article 66 in an urgent procedure.

263. The substantive examination of the patent application is conducted in:

(1) one of the selected institutions, which as a rule are national or international offices and which on the basis of PCT have a status of authorized institutions for international search or preliminary international examination of international patent applications; or
(2) one of the institutions with which a special agreement is signed for the purpose of searching and substantive examination.

264. The evidence of the substantive examination serves to determine if the invention fully meets all the conditions for granting the patent right. This will be the case if the subject of the application is an invention that:

– may be protected by a patent;[28]
– is described in a manner that an expert in the field may apply it;[29]
– complies with the rule of unity of invention;[30] and
– is new,[31] has inventive step,[32] and is applicable in industry.[33]

265. The Office takes its decision on the basis of the presented evidence from the substantive examination and on the basis of additional examination. The additional examination is to determine whether the requirements for granting of patent have been satisfied, specifically whether the subject of the application is in compliance with the requirement that the application can prima facie be protected by a patent (Article 56, paragraph (1) item 5). The Office may not take a decision if it previously had not notified in writing the applicant about the reasons for which it cannot grant the right as a whole or partially and if it failed to invite the applicant to respond within a reasonable time limit, which may be extended up to six months on the basis of a justified request by the applicant.

28. In accordance with Arts 25 and 26.
29. In accordance with Art. 27, para. (2).
30. Art. 35.
31. Arts 27 and 28.
32. Art. 29.
33. Art. 30.

266. On the basis of the presented evidence, the Office shall determine to what extent the contents and scope of the patent claims regarding the invention meet the conditions of novelty, inventive step and applicability in industry (Articles 27, 29, and 30), and shall issue one of the following decisions:

(1) decision that the invention meets all the conditions referred to in Articles 27, 29, and 30 and that the patent claim or patent claims are fully in compliance with those conditions;
(2) decision that the invention only partially meets the conditions referred to in Articles 27, 29, and 30, which provides limited further validity of the patent claim or patent claims in a scope that fulfils the conditions; or
(3) decision to announce nullity when the invention, as of the date of filing the patent application, does not fulfil the conditions referred to in Articles 27, 29, and 30.

IV. Patent Register, Publication and Patent Certificate (Articles 67–70)

267. The data from the decision for grant of patent, together with the publishing date and number, are entered in the register of patents maintained by the Office. The data from the decision rejecting the patent application are recorded in the register of patent applications. Any changes relating to the applicant, the right holder and the right itself are recorded in both the register of patent applications and the Patent Register. The changes recorded in the Patent Register are published in the official journal of the Office.

268. The data from the decision for patent granting are published in the official journal of the Office within ninety days from the date of adoption of the decision. The invention abstract shall be published together with the data on the decision adopted on the basis of partial examination. The first patent claim shall be published together with the data of the decision issued on the basis of full examination, and the number of other patent claims shall be stated.

269. The Office shall issue to the holder of a patent right a certificate within six months from the date of the decision for grant of a patent. At the request of the patent holder, the Office shall issue a patent specification.

V. Confidential Patent (Articles 71–73)

270. The applications for grant of a patent relating to defence are deemed confidential and are filed to the Minister for Defence. The provisions of the LIP apply in the process of patent granting with regard to confidential inventions, unless otherwise provided. If during the examination process of the filed application, the Minister for Defence finds that the invention is not confidential, the application shall be forwarded to the Office. And if during the examination procedure of the application, the Office finds the invention to be confidential, it shall forward the application to the Minister for Defence. If the Minister for Defence finds that the invention has ceased to be confidential, the complete file will be submitted to the Office. After receiving the file, the Office shall enter the patent in the register of patents and shall issue the patent holder a patent certificate or a specification and publish the data.

271. The Ministry of Defence shall have the exclusive right to use the confidential invention and dispose of that invention. The holder of the right shall be entitled to a one-time compensation for confidential invention which is protected with a patent, regardless if and to which extent the invention is used for the needs of defence. The amount of the compensation is determined by mutual agreement by the right holder and the Minister for Defence. In case agreement is not reached, the holder of the patent right, in accordance with the rules of non-contentious procedure, may request from the court to determine the amount of the compensation.

272. The confidential patent has specific properties that are regulated in the LIP. The patent related to a confidential invention shall not be published. National legal and natural persons may request protection of a confidential invention abroad only on the basis of a written approval by the Minister for Defence. The rules relating to confidential patents apply accordingly to applications for grant of patents for inventions of interest to the state security, for which the Minister for Interior decides. The Government prescribes which inventions are considered as confidential, as well as the method of patent granting for such inventions.

§5. Ownership and Transfer (Assignment – Licences)

273. The LIP defines the concepts of inventor and successor in title. An inventor is the natural person that has created the invention in the course of his creative work (Article 32). The LIP also specifies who cannot be considered an inventor – the person who in the creation of the invention has provided only technical assistance. Inventor's successor in title is a legal or natural person entitled to acquire a patent right by virtue of law, legal deed, inheritance or court decision (Article 33). The employer is considered to be inventor's successor in title where by virtue of law or employment contract, he has the right to acquire patent for invention created in the course of the inventor's employment. An educational and research institution where the innovation has been created, as a result of innovation or development activity, where it is financed from the Budget of the Republic of Macedonia according to the Law on Innovation Activity, is considered a legal successor, unless otherwise agreed prior to the commencement of the project.

274. According to Article 271 of the LIP, the patent right applicant and the holder of the right may transfer his right in its entirety or in part, by agreement, in accordance with the applicable laws. The transfer agreement must be composed in writing and the signatures of the contracting parties certified by notary public; otherwise, it shall not produce any legal effect. At the request of any contracting party, the agreement is registered in the register kept in the Office; otherwise, it shall not produce legal effect against third parties.

275. The LIP contains provisions on a licence agreement in Article 272. The applicant of the patent right and the holder of the right may transfer that right for use by licence agreement, in accordance with the LIP or other regulations. The licence agreement must be composed in writing; otherwise, it does not produce any legal effect. If several persons have submitted a patent application or if the patent holders are several entities, the consent of all these persons is necessary for concluding the licence agreement. If there is no consent, the rules of co-ownership apply to the transfer of the right to usage. At the request of one of the contracting parties, the licence agreement shall be registered in the register kept in the Office. If it is not registered, it shall not have effect against third parties.

276. According to Article 273, a provision of the licence agreement shall be void if it sets limitations to the licence user which do not result from the right that is subject to the agreement or if it is not necessary for keeping that right, or if it is contrary to the regulations relating to competition.

277. In addition to these specific provisions on the transfer of rights in the LIP, the Law on Obligations as a *lex generalis* applies to the agreements for transfer and licence, as stipulated in Article 274.

§6. Scope of Exclusive Rights

278. According to the LIP, Article 89, the holder of a patent has the exclusive right:

(1) to use the protected invention in production;
(2) to place on the market items manufactured according to the protected invention, and
(3) to dispose of the patent.

279. The patent holder is entitled to prohibit the use of the protected invention in the production or in trade by third parties that do not have a licence for such use if such a use relates to production, offering for sale, export, or import and storage of products for those purposes.

280. These provisions also apply to patents in the field of biotechnology which are regulated separately in Article 90. Specifically, they apply to any biological material with specific characteristics as a result of the invention, and shall be extended to the biological material derived from that biological material by propagation or multiplication in an identical or in a divergent form and having the same characteristics.

281. The patent holder is entitled to prohibit another person from offering and supplying, without his consent, products which constitute essential elements of the invention if the person has known or should have known based on the circumstances of the case that the product was intended for someone else's invention. This also applies to a product containing or comprised of genetic information and shall extend to all biological materials in which genetic information is contained and perform their functions, with the exception of the materials referred to in Article 25, paragraph (5).

282. The exclusive right also applies to a patent protecting a procedure or the product derived directly from that procedure. It also applies to the procedure of producing biological material with specific characteristics as a result of the invention and shall be extended to the biological material derived directly from that procedure and from any biological material derived from the biological material by propagation or multiplication in an identical or a divergent form and having the same characteristics.

283. If the patent is granted for procedure (Article 92), its effect shall extend to the products and materials directly obtained through that procedure. In case of a lack of evidence to the contrary, the product shall be considered as obtained through a protected procedure if the product is new, or if there is a reasonable doubt that the product is obtained through a protected procedure and that the holder of a patent was not in a position, despite the reasonable effort made, to determine the procedure that was used. There is a reasonable doubt that the product has been obtained through a protected procedure if the protected procedure is the only known procedure. The burden of proof shall rest with the alleged infringer.

284. The scope of exclusive rights of the patent holder shall be determined in accordance with the text of the patent claims that are finally accepted in the patent granting procedure where the description and the drawings serve to interpret the patent claims (Article 93).

§7. Limitations and Exceptions to the Scope of Patent Protection – Compulsory Licences

I. Limitations and Exceptions

285. The LIP in Article 91 provides for situations that represent free use. The right of the patent holder regarding the exclusive utilization of the invention shall not relate to:

(1) utilization of the invention for personal and non-commercial purposes;
(2) undertaking activities for research and development of the subject of the protected invention, in particular: manufacture, use, offer for sale, export or import of the protected invention, including activities for obtaining approval for placing medications for human and veterinary medicine and products for protection of plants on the market; and
(3) direct and individual preparation of the medicine in a pharmacy on the basis of an individual medical prescription and to procedures which relate to the prepared medicine.

286. Article 94 provides for an exception based on previous use of the invention. The patent right will not have an effect on the person which prior to the filing date of the application or prior to the date of the recognized priority right has used the invention conscientiously and not in public in the Republic of Macedonia, or has prepared everything necessary for its use. That person has the right, without the consent of the holder of the patent, to continue the utilization of the invention to the extent it has utilized or prepared it until the date of filing the patent application.

287. Pursuant to Article 95, it shall not be considered as infringement of the exclusive rights to the patent holder if the subject of the invention relates to products manufactured according to the patent when used in the construction or the equipment of ships, aircraft or land vehicles that belong to any of the states of the Paris Union or the WTO, if such a means of transportation is temporarily or suddenly in the territory of the Republic of Macedonia, provided that the mounted product serves exclusively for the needs of that vehicle.

288. There is also an exemption from the infringement of patent right in the field of biotechnology (Article 96). The person using the plant material for propagation, on the basis of the consent by the patent holder, shall not infringe the right relating to the selling or other types of commercial exploitation of plant material for propagation if the product of their own harvest is used for propagation and multiplication for their own needs and for the needs of their own property. The person that uses the cattle or other animal reproductive material, on the basis of the consent of the patent holder, shall not infringe the right relating to the selling or other types of commercial exploitation if the protected cattle is used for agricultural activities, including reproduction of animals and production of other animal reproductive material for the purposes of their agricultural activity, but not for commercial reproductive purposes.

II. Compulsory Licences

289. Compulsory licences are regulated in the LIP in Articles 97–115. As a rule, if the patent holder does not use the invention protected by a patent or uses it in a scope which is insufficient to meet the needs of the national market, and refuses to enter into a licence agreement or sets non-market conditions for entering into that contract, the right to use the invention may be assigned by a compulsory licence to another person, with the obligation to pay a compensation to the patent holder. The request for a compulsory licence may not be submitted prior to the expiry of a period of four years from the date of filing the patent application or prior to the expiry of a period of three years from the date of the patent granting, whichever is later.

290. Compulsory licence may also be issued if the utilization of the invention protected by a patent is necessary due to emergency situations in the country, protection of public interest in the area of health, food, protection and promotion of the environment or if it is of particular interest to a certain industrial field or if it is necessary for implementing a judicial or administrative procedure related to protection of competition. In this case, the compulsory licence may be issued even prior to the expiry of the period specified above.

291. A compulsory licence will not be issued if the patent holder proves that there are legal constraints which justify the fact that the invention protected by a patent has not been used or has been insufficiently used.

292. Article 98 covers the particularities of the compulsory licence. The compulsory licence may not be exclusive. The licence shall be valid as long as the reason for which it has been issued lasts. On the basis of a justified request of the interested person, the compulsory licence shall be cancelled if the reasons for which it was issued cease to exist, and there is no possibility for those reasons to occur again, provided that the legitimate rights of the assignee/acquirer of the licence are protected. The compulsory licence may not be transferred, unless the transfer is done together with the production capacity or with part of it where the invention for which the licence has been issued is used. Compulsory licence is issued for the needs of the national market, unless it is proved in legal proceedings that this is contrary to the protection of competition on the market.

293. When a compulsory licence is issued, the patent holder is entitled to an adequate compensation. The amount of the compensation is set out with an agreement between the patent holder and the user who has been given the licence or who uses the invention protected by a patent. The amount is adequate to the value of the economic licence and the need for harmonization with the procedure for protection of competition. If an agreement on the amount of the compensation cannot be reached, the court shall determine the amount of the compensation. The user who has been given the licence shall not be prevented from using the invention in the absence of an agreement or a court decision.

294. A compulsory licence may also be issued if the invention protected by a patent cannot be used as a whole or partially without using another invention protected by a former patent, whereby the later invention, representing a more significant technical improvement, is of particular importance to the economy or to fulfilling the public needs. In this case, the holder of the previous patent may request a compulsory licence for the use of the invention of the latter patent for an adequate compensation.

295. The court competent for settling disputes concerning industrial property rights in legal proceedings shall decide on the issuing of compulsory licences. The procedure to issue a compulsory licence is initiated with a lawsuit against the holder of a patent or of a supplementary protection certificate, which contains a request for issuing compulsory licence. In the procedure for issuing compulsory licence, the person registered in the Patent Register is considered as a patent holder.

296. There are also provisions on the compulsory licence for the needs of public health. Any person that has filed a request in compliance with the provisions of the LIP may be issued, by the court, a compulsory patent licence or a supplementary protection certificate for the needs of production and sale of pharmaceutical products, where such products are intended to be exported in importing countries with problems in public health. When deciding on issuing compulsory licence, the court shall take into consideration the WTO General Council Decision of 30 August 2003 on the implementation of paragraph 6 of the Doha Declaration on the TRIPS Agreement and public health of 14 November 2001 (WTO Decision). The pharmaceutical product in this context means any product in the pharmaceutical industry, including medications for human use, which include any substance or mixture of substances designed for treatment or prevention of human diseases including any substance or mixture of substances which may be applied to people in terms of renewal, improvement, or adjustment of their physiological functions by causing pharmaceutical, immunological, or metabolic effects or by giving medical diagnosis, including active components and diagnostic devices used outside the alive human body.

297. Importing country is defined in the LIP as any country in which pharmaceutical products are exported and it can be:

(1) any least developed country stated as such in the list of the United Nations (UN);
(2) any WTO member, except the least developed Member State referred to in item (1), which has sent a notification to the TRIPS Council on the intention to use the system as an importing country, either as a whole or partially;
(3) any country, which is not a WTO member, and which has been listed by the Development Assistance Committee of the Organization for Economic Cooperation and Development (OECD) as a country with low income of gross national product per capita of less than USD 745 and for which the Ministry of Economy is notified about the intention to use the system as an import country, regardless of whether it will use the system in this way as a whole or partially.

298. If a WTO Member State has given a statement that it will not use this right, then it does not fulfil the requirements to use the system as an importing country. The importing countries that are not WTO members, and are the least developed countries or developing countries that fulfil the requirements above, must fulfil the following additional requirements:

(1) the importing country is obliged to send a notification directly to the Ministry of Economy;
(2) the importing country is obliged to state in the notification that it will use the system to resolve public health problems, and will not use it as a means for achieving industrial and commercial goals, and that it will apply the measures referred to in item 4 of the WTO Decision. If the country fails to comply with this requirement, the court may repeal the compulsory licence on the basis of a lawsuit initiated by the right holder or the Ministry of Economy.

299. The lawsuit that includes a request for issuing a compulsory licence for the needs of the public health can be initiated in the court if there is a patent or a supplementary protection certificate in the territory of the Republic of Macedonia that covers the works for production and sale for the purpose of exporting. The party initiating the lawsuit for compulsory licence is obliged to attach the following to the lawsuit:

(1) applications for compulsory licences in other countries for the same product, with data on the quantities and the importing countries;
(2) the applicant for compulsory licence, and in case there is an agent, data about the agent;
(3) name of the pharmaceutical product that is not subject to protection, which the applicant plans to produce on the basis of compulsory licence;
(4) quantity of the pharmaceutical product that the applicant plans to produce on the basis of compulsory licence;
(5) data on the importing country;
(6) evidence about previous negotiations with the right holder; and
(7) evidence about the application of the authorized representative of the importing country or the nongovernmental organization which operates with an authorization from one or more importing countries or UN bodies or another international health organization which operates with an authorization of one or more importing countries, indicating the quantity of the required product.

300. Compulsory licence may be issued only if within a period of thirty days prior to submitting the lawsuit, the applicant has unsuccessfully tried to get a consent from the right holder to utilize the protected invention under reasonable market conditions and terms. This provision does not apply in case of necessity or other circumstance of emergency in the country or in case of other public non-commercial use, in compliance with Article 31, item b) of the TRIPS Agreement.

301. The court will notify without delay the right holder about the application filed for granting a compulsory licence and shall provide him an opportunity to make a statement.

302. The compulsory licence for the needs of public health has certain properties. The licence may not be exclusive. Its duration and scope stated in the court decision issuing the licence shall depend solely on the duration of the reason due to which it had been issued. The quantity of products that may be produced on the basis of the compulsory licence must not exceed the quantity which is necessary to respond to the needs of the importing countries stated in the lawsuit, taking into consideration the quantity of products produced in other countries on the basis of compulsory licence. The licence may be transferred only together with the production capacity or with the part of it in which the invention for which compulsory licence has been issued is used.

303. The product which is produced or imported on the basis of a compulsory licence for the needs of public health may not be offered for sale or placed on the market of a country not indicated in the application, except when the importing country, in compliance with item 6, sub item (i) of the WTO Decision, exports to a country that has also signed the regional trade agreement and has the same problem in the field of health. The packaging or any relevant text must contain a clear indication that the product is a subject to a compulsory licence, the name of the court granting the licence and the number of the file, a clear indication that the product is intended exclusively for export and distribution in the importing country or countries and detailed data regarding the product intended for customs authorities in the Republic of Macedonia. The compulsory licence is issued for the needs of the local market, unless proved in the judicial procedure that this is contrary to the protection of competition on the market. If the product for which in the Republic of Macedonia a compulsory licence has been issued is protected with patent in the importing country indicated in the application, the product may be exported only if that country has issued a compulsory licence for import, sale, and/or distribution of that product. The conditions under which the licence is issued shall not affect the method of distribution in the importing country.

304. When deciding on the application for issuing compulsory licence, the court shall check if:

(1) every importing country, member of the WTO and stated in the application, has sent a notification to the WTO in compliance with the decision, or if every importing country, which is not member of the WTO and is stated in the application, has notified the Ministry of Economy for each product from the application regardless of the possibility granted to the least developed countries with the decision;
(2) the product quantity stated in the application does not exceed that which the importing country has notified to the WTO or the Ministry of Economy;
(3) the total quantity of products for which production is authorized with regard to any importing country has not significantly exceeded the quantity which that country has notified to the WTO or the Ministry of Economy, taking into consideration the other granted compulsory licences.

305. The court decision shall state the production activities for which the applicant shall be authorized, and which are necessary for production, export, and distribution in the country or countries stated in the application.

306. The court decision shall order the products to be clearly marked with special labels or indications that they are produced on the basis of a compulsory licence so that they differ from those produced by the right holder, by using special packaging or special colours and shapes, if such a difference is possible and does not have a big impact on the price. The court shall order the licensee prior to the delivery in the importing country, to put information on the website concerning the quantity of products that he supplies the importing countries with, as well as the way of labelling those products, and to notify the Ministry of Economy and the Ministry of

Health about the website. On the basis of the proposal by the right holder for securing evidence, the court may pronounce a measure to make inspection in the working books and other documents for licence, in order to check if all the obligations from the decision to issue a compulsory licence are met, in particular, to check the product's final destination, whereby the working books and documents must contain evidence on export of the product in the form of an export declaration that has been inspected by the customs, as well as import evidence.

307. In its decision, the court shall order the applicant to pay compensation to the right holder, which is determined in case of a serious danger to human health or other circumstances in case of urgent necessity or public non-commercial use laid down in Article 31 (b) of TRIPS Agreement. The compensation shall amount to a maximum of 4% of the total price paid by the importing countries or which is paid for the benefit of such a country. This provision is treated as an exception, whereas in all other cases, the compensation shall be established by taking into consideration the economic values of the use for which the respective country or the importing countries are authorized, as well as the humanitarian and non-commercial circumstances regarding the issue of a licence.

308. The court shall reject the request for a compulsory licence if it does not include the elements necessary for taking the decision or if the conditions for granting the licence are not fulfilled. The court shall not take the decision if it has not previously called the applicant to respond to the reasons for which the court is not able to issue the licence.

309. The right holder or the licensee has the right to initiate a lawsuit and ask the court to revoke the compulsory licence if it finds out that the opposite party does not respect the decision for issuing a compulsory licence. In the judgment for termination of the compulsory licence, the court shall define a deadline in which the licensee is obliged, at its own expense, to repurpose all the products in its ownership or responsibility or to allow the importing country to do so or otherwise remove them, in agreement with the right holder. When the importing country gives a notification that the quantity of pharmaceutical products has become insufficient to meet its need, the licensee may file a lawsuit and ask for change of the conditions for issuing a licence, for the purpose of production and export of additional quantities of products to the level of the quantities required to meet the needs of the importing country. In such cases, the court proceeds urgently. If the required quantity of the product does not exceed 25% of the total quantity allocated by the basic licence, the notification requirement (Article 109 paragraph 1 item 1) shall not be applied.

310. The court shall inform, through the Ministry of Economy, the TRIPS Council about the effective decisions for the issuance of a compulsory licence, the conditions under which it has been issued, its termination and modification. It will submit the following data: name and address of the licensee; the product subject to the licence; provided quantity; importing country; duration of the licence; address of the website.

311. It is prohibited to import products in the Republic of Macedonia subject to compulsory licence as regulated in the LIP for the purpose of free distribution, reimport, suspension procedures or placing into free zone or free warehouse. This does not apply in case of re-export in the importing country stated in the application and identified on the packaging and the supporting documents for the product, or of a procedure at customs or transit warehouse or in free zone or free warehouse for the purpose of re-export in the importing country.

312. If there is a ground to suspect that the products produced on the basis of the compulsory licence issued in accordance with the provisions of the LIP are imported on the territory of the Republic of Macedonia, the customs authorities shall retain for checking the concrete products as long as necessary, but up to ten working days at the most. In case of special circumstances, the customs authorities may decide to extend the deadline for additional ten working days. They shall, without delay, inform the right holder and the producer or exporter of these products about the retention, and shall invite them to submit data and evidence for the products. If customs authorities, within the period of retention, find out that there is infringement of the compulsory licence, contrary to the prohibition on import, they shall confiscate the products and withdraw them from the market, in accordance with the customs regulations. Procedure for retention and confiscation shall be at the expense of the importer, in accordance with the customs regulations. Any other person, which has tried to make unlawful import, shall be held responsible for the costs jointly with the importer. If it is established that the import of the retained products is an infringement of the prohibition and if the customs regulations have been respected, the customs authorities shall place the products on the market in the territory of the Republic of Macedonia. The customs authorities report to the Ministry of Economy on the confiscation and destruction of products.

§8. Duration of Protection – Maintaining and Termination of Patent Protection

313. The patent validity in the Macedonian LIP is aligned with international rules. Pursuant to Article 74, the patent right is valid for twenty years, counting from the date of filing the application. The validity of the patent may be extended beyond the twenty years, for no more than five years, in case when the subject matter of the patent is a medical product, product for plant protection, or a process through which they are produced, for which, prior to placing them on the market, an administrative procedure of authorization, laid down by law, needs to be conducted. If the patent right is obtained on the basis of the decision taken after a partial examination, it shall be valid for ten years from the date of filing the application.

314. Several provisions (Article 75–85) govern in more detail the extended protection beyond twenty years. The patent right validity may be extended by issuing a certificate. The certificate is issued if on the date of submitting the request in the Republic of Macedonia:

(1) there is a valid basic patent for the product;
(2) the product has been placed on the market on the basis of approval issued in accordance with the regulations on the placing of medicines on the market or regulations on the placing of products for plant protection on the market;
(3) the product previously has not been subject to a certificate, or there is no previously issued certificate for the same product as a medical product or as products for protection of plants; and
(4) the approval laid down in item (2) is the first approval for placing the product on the market of the Republic of Macedonia as a medical product or as products for protection of plants.

315. The certificate is issued for a product protected by a basic patent for which there is an approval for placing on the market and using a medical product or a product for plant protection, prior to the expiry of the certificate. The right for which the certificate has been issued shall be identical to the right of the basic patent and shall be subject to the same limitations and obligations as the basic patent.

316. Beneficiaries of the right of the certificate are the holder of the basic patent or its legal successor. In case of several holders of the basic patent, the procedure for issuing the certificate may be initiated by the joint representative or any of the holders upon prior consent of the other holders or of their legal successor.

317. The procedure for issuing a certificate is initiated by submitting a request for obtaining a certificate to the Office. The request shall be filed within six months after the date when the first approval for placing the product on the market of the Republic of Macedonia has been issued, or within six months from the date of granting of the basic patent, if the approval to place the product on the market has been issued prior to the granting of the basic patent.

318. There is a specific form for submitting the request. The approval for placing the product on the market within the Republic of Macedonia, issued by the competent authority, shall be attached to the request, together with other documents and attachments.

319. The Office conducts a procedure of formal examination, where it examines if the request includes the constituent elements and attachments and other formal elements, and if the request is filed within the prescribed deadline. If the request was not filed in compliance with this provision, the Office shall invite the applicant to correct the shortcomings within a period of sixty days, counting from the date of receiving the invitation. The time limit may be extended for additional sixty days in case of a justified request by the applicant. If the applicant fails to correct the shortcomings, the Office shall reject the request.

320. Next, the Office conducts the examination procedure for issuing a certificate, where it examines if on the date of filing the request the conditions for issuing a certificate have been fulfilled. If the Office finds that the conditions have been fulfilled, it shall notify the applicant within a period of thirty days to pay the costs for publication of the certificate in the official journal of the Office, and the fee for validity maintenance. If the applicant pays the costs and the fee, the Office shall issue a decision for a certificate; otherwise, the Office shall reject the request.

321. The certificate starts to be valid upon the expiry of the legally prescribed period of validity of the basic patent, for a period equal to the time between the date of filing the application for a basic patent and the date of receiving the approval for placing the product on the market of the Republic of Macedonia, but reduced for five years.

322. In case the conditions have not been met, or the request has not been filed by an authorized person, the Office shall notify the applicant in writing of the reasons for which the certificate may not be issued and shall invite the applicant to respond to those reasons within a time limit that cannot be longer than six months. In case the applicant fails to respond, the Office shall reject the request.

323. In the procedure of granting and maintenance of the patent right, fees and charges are due (Article 86). The annual fees for maintaining the validity of the patent right and the certificate are paid counting from the date of filing the patent application. The annual fee shall be paid by the beginning of the year for which the fee is paid or by the date of filing the application. The fees and charges may be paid by anyone without the approval of the agent.

324. Pursuant to Article 87, the patent right shall cease to be valid prior to the expiry of the validity period in the following cases:

(1) if the prescribed fees are not paid – from the day after the date of missing the deadline for payment;
(2) if the holder waives the right – the day after the date of filing the waiving request to the Office;
(3) on the basis of a court decision or decision of the Office in the cases provided for in the LIP – on the date set out in the decision; and
(4) if the legal person that is a holder of the patent right has ceased its operations – on the date of termination; or if the natural person which is a holder of the patent right has died – on the date of death, or if a disappeared person which is a holder of the patent right is proclaimed dead – on the date when the decision becomes legally effective, unless that right has been assigned to the successors of the legal person or of the natural person.

325. The Office shall decide to terminate the validity of the patent if these conditions occur.

326. Under Article 88, if a licence, a pledge or another right in favour of a third party is entered in the register of patents, the patent holder may not waive his rights without a consent in writing by that third person. If the patent holder fails to pay the prescribed fee within the specified period, and a licence, a pledge or another right is entered in the register in favour of a third person, the Office shall notify that person that the fee has not been paid and that that person may pay it within six months from the date of the notification in order to keep the registered right. In case of a dispute regarding the securing of registered rights of a third party, the court, if necessary for the securing of those rights, may decide the patent right to be assigned to the person under the name of which the licence, the pledge, or another right has been registered, until the fulfilment of the obligations.

§9. Infringement and Remedies

327. The rules regarding judicial protection for infringement of the patent right are covered in Part X of the LIP (Articles 291–315) and apply to all the rights falling under the scope of the Law. As a general rule, according to Article 291, the person whose right is infringed is entitled to protection of the right by submitting a lawsuit to the court with competence to settle disputes on industrial property rights. Infringement of the registered and recognized rights is any unauthorized use, disposal, limitation, imitation, association, rights disturbance and the like, contrary to the provisions of the Law. Imitation occurs if the average consumer of goods or services, regardless of the type of products, may notice the difference only if he pays special attention.

328. The following persons are entitled, according to Article 292, to initiate a lawsuit relating to patent protection:

- the submitter of the application for protection of right;
- the holder of the right;
- the licensee of the exclusive licence, in scope in which he acquired the right to use, on the basis of a legal deed or law.

329. When a right is infringed, each of the holders of that right may in respect of any third party demand protection of the right as if he was a single holder. When a person infringing the right fulfils the claims of one of the holders of the right, its obligation towards the other right holders shall cease. In case of ongoing legal proceedings, the holders of the same right shall be deemed as a single party in the litigation.

330. The content of the lawsuit is specified in Article 294. The person whose right is infringed may demand from the court:

(1) To determine the infringement of the right.
(2) To ban the actions set in the lawsuit that are infringing the right.
(3) To claim compensation for damages caused by infringement of rights intentionally or by negligence. The rules on obligations apply in such cases.
(4) To confiscate or destroy the products produced or in circulation by infringement of the right and means used for their production. The court applies the principle of proportionality when considering this claim.

(5) To order the defendant to provide information about the identity of third parties involved in production and distribution of goods or services infringing the rights, as well as about their distribution channels.
(6) To submit the documentation and the data about the person infringing the right.
(7) Civil penalty, in case of intention or gross negligence.
(8) Publication of the judgment at the expense of the defendant.
(9) Other claims. In the case of patents, the inventor, his successor or other legal successor may request from the court during the validity period of the patent to declare him as the holder of the patent if the patent is issued under the name of a person who is not the inventor, his successor or other legal successor. The inventor of the patent may also request to be specified in the application and all the other documents, and following his death this claim can be made by his successors. In this case, the lawsuit may be initiated from the date of filing the application form as well as during the whole time of validity of the patent.

331. The lawsuit may be filed within three years from the date when the plaintiff becomes aware of the infringement and the infringer, and in any case no later than five years from the date of the infringement. The procedure is urgent. The regulations on civil litigation procedure and on securing claims apply in the proceedings for protection of rights. The court may suspend the procedure relating to infringement of the right of a filed patent until a decision for granting the right is adopted by the Office.

332. Within ninety days of the date of delivering the legally effective judgment accepting the lawsuit claims, the plaintiff may request to be registered in the relevant register as a holder of the right and to be issued the appropriate document by the Office. If the person does not submit a request for the granted right, the right shall be deleted from the relevant register.

333. The rights the third party has acquired from the former holder of the rights shall be valid for the new holder of the rights if they were registered in the relevant register or were duly reported for registration prior to the commencement of the dispute.

334. In case when the person provides evidence that his right has been infringed or will be infringed, the court upon his proposal may determine temporary measures to secure his requests as follows:

- prohibit all infringing activities and their continuation;
- confiscate, remove from circulation and keep samples, means, equipment and related documents; and
- adopt other similar measures.

335. In addition, when the infringement is done while performing business activities for the purpose of gaining financial benefit and such infringement may cause irreparable harm, the court may set as a guarantee the confiscation of movable and immovable assets owned by the defendant and assets that are not directly related to the infringement, as well as a ban for disposing of finances on the accounts in financial institutions or disposing of other property.

336. If requested by the person whose right is infringed or there is justified doubt that his right will be infringed, the court may order a measure for providing evidence, especially regarding:

- preparation of a detailed description of the goods that have likely infringed the right with or without taking a sample;
- confiscation of the goods which is believed to have infringed the right;
- confiscation of materials and means used for preparation and distribution of goods believed to infringe the right, as well as related documentation.

337. When the party in the legal procedure relies on evidence and claims that that evidence is with the opposing party or under its control, the court shall invite the opposing party to provide such evidence specifying the time limit for submitting it. Where the party invited to provide evidence denies that they have the evidence or that it is under their control, the court may present evidence for determining the facts.

338. In addition to the civil protection, the right holder can request inspection relating to the circulation and use of protected industrial property rights, done by the State Market Inspectorate (Articles 317–320). The Inspectorate can take a range of measures, including seizing infringing products, prohibiting the use of infringing means and equipment, and issuing to the infringing party a temporary suspension of business activities. The LIP contains provisions on misdemeanours and corresponding sanctions, primarily fines (Articles 321–322v).

§10. Overlapping and Relation to Other Intellectual Property Laws

339. Patent right is one of the industrial property rights regulated with the LIP. As such, many of the provisions in the Law, such as those on transfer and licensing, or on judicial protection, apply to all the rights within scope. In addition, the body competent for registering all industrial property rights is the State Industrial Property Office, and the policymaking authority in this field is the Ministry of Economy which prepares the legislation relating to patents and other industrial property rights.

340. Patents can potentially have overlap with copyright when it comes to computer programs.According to the Macedonian legal system, computer programs are clearly considered as copyright works, and protected under copyright rules. Computer programs in themselves cannot enjoy patent protection, as the LIP explicitly excludes them from the notion of invention.

Chapter 3. Trademarks

§1. Sources – Legislation

341. The following international conventions and agreements regarding trademarks are part of Macedonian legislation on trademarks: Madrid Agreement concerning the international registration of marks (1891);[34] Nice Agreement concerning the international classification of goods and services for the purposes of the registration of marks (1957);[35] the Convention Establishing the WIPO (1967);[36] the Vienna Agreement establishing an international classification of the figurative elements of marks (1973);[37] the Nairobi treaty on the protection of the Olympic symbol (1981);[38,39] the Protocol to the Madrid Agreement (1989);[40] Agreement on Trade-Related Aspects of Intellectual Property Rights (TRIPS Agreement) (1994);[41] and the Singapore Treaty on the law of trademarks (TLT) (2006).[42]

342. The current Macedonian trademark legislation framework is mostly part of the LIP,[43] particularly its Chapter II, as well as the Rulebook on Trademarks, enacted by the Industrial Property Protection Office.[44] According to LIP, Article 3, 'Trademark' (mark for goods, service mark, collective, and certification mark) is defined as industrial property right acquired in a procedure in compliance with LIP and which protects the trade sign.[45] The Law on the Protection of Competition (LPC) is also relevant.[46]

§2. Subject Matter of Protection

I. Signs Which May Serve as Trademarks

343. According to the LIP, signs that may be represented graphically and which are capable for distinguishing goods or services of one undertaking from those of

34. Notification of succession by the Republic of Macedonia: 23 Jul. 1993.
35. Notification of succession by the Republic of Macedonia: 23 Jul. 1993.
36. Notification of succession by the Republic of Macedonia: 23 Jul. 1993.
37. Notification of succession, 10 Mar. 1994. Official Journal of the Republic of Macedonia No. 19/2010.
38. Official Journal of the Republic of Macedonia, No. 165/2013.
39. Declaration/Notification of Succession: 23 Jul. 1993.
40. Official Journal of the Republic of Macedonia, No. 12/2002.
41. Official Journal of the Republic of Macedonia, No. 07/03.
42. Official Journal of the Republic of Macedonia, No. 19/10.
43. Official Journal 21/09, 24/11, 12/14, 41/14, 152/15, 53/16, 83/18, 31/20.
44. Official Journal of the Republic of Macedonia No. 92/2009.
45. *See* LIP, Art. 175.
46. Official Journal of the Republic of Macedonia No. 80/99.

other undertakings may be protected by trademarks, such as: words, letters, numerals, pictures, drawings, combinations of colours, three-dimensional forms, including shapes of goods or their packaging, as well as combinations of all the above-mentioned signs. The words and letters referred to may be written in any language and alphabet.

344. Concerning the distinctiveness, LIP states that a sign shall be capable of distinguishing if it gives to certain goods or services comparing them with the identical or similar goods or services, a special distinctive character. Furthermore, while establishing whether a given sign is capable of distinguishing, all circumstances shall be taken into consideration, particularly the time and scope of its past use in trade.

II. Different Categories of Marks

345. From a theoretical aspect, Macedonian intellectual property legislation adopts the basic formulations of the classification of trademarks, which has the trademark holder as a referent criterion for classification of certain legal institutes in the circumstances when there is a 'pluralism of the subjects'.[47] Consequently, the Macedonian legislation categorizes trademarks into three types: individual, collective and certification.

346. The individual mark represents a mark in a narrower sense of the word, and it entails the 'classical case' of a mark whose holder is a legal entity. Hence, the collective and certification mark are specific forms of the mark, i.e., marks for which the basic rules for individual marks apply, with certain specificities.[48]

347. In this sense, LIP is in line with the concept that unlike the individual mark which protects the rights of only one person, the collective mark protects the rights of more (mostly legal) persons, who have regulated the alleged right with the general act for the collective mark. Additionally, the members of the entity (association or similar) are obligated to use the collective mark only for designating goods or services which correspond to specified technical and other characteristics. As for the registration procedure, in most legislations, the application for the collective mark must be accompanied by a copy of the rules determining the use of the collective mark.[49]

348. In other words, according to Article 219 of LIP, collective mark shall protect a sign intended for collective designation of the goods or services put on the

47. Examples of other legal institutes include the theoretical concept of ownership and the collective ownership in property law or the obligations with complex parties in the law of obligations and the cases of co-authorship and collective acquirement of copyright and related rights. *See* Y. Reboul, M. Polenak Akimovska, G. Naumovski: Introduction to Trademarks and Geographical Indications, Tempus project 144582, Faculty of Law Iustinianus Primus, Skopje, 2010, p. 10.
48. *Ibid.*
49. *Ibid.*

market by an association of legal and natural persons-right-owners. In this sense, an applicant for collective mark may be a domestic association of legal and natural right-owners. Also, in compliance with the international conventions, which have been ratified by the Republic of Macedonia, applicant for collective mark may also be a foreign legal right-owner.[50] It should be noted that any change or amendment of the agreement regulating the use of a collective mark made on a request of the applicant or the owner of a collective mark results in its registration by State Office of Industrial Property (SOIP). Collective marks regulations also stipulate that the rights arising from a collective mark shall not be transferable and shall not be the subject matter of the licence.[51]

349. Concerning the certification mark, LIP defines it as mark that protects a sign which is being used by several companies under supervision of the certification mark owner, and it shall protect the quality, origin, way of production and other joint characteristics of goods or services of those companies.[52] The application for certification mark shall be accompanied by rules for use of the certification mark containing provisions on the quality and other characteristics of the goods or services, the control measures that will be used by the applicant of the certification mark and the sanctions he/she will be applying. The holder of the right to certification mark may not use that mark for designating products and services that he/she puts on the market.[53]

§3. Conditions of Protection

350. As noted in Macedonian intellectual property theory, the LIP approach on the absolute and relative grounds for rejecting a trademark registration reiterates two points: (1) the absolute grounds for refusal of the registration of a sign are in function of the protection of the public interest and refer to all signs, regardless of the goods and services they indicate, and the institution in charge of the absolute reasons for rejections is the SOIP, by official duty; (2) the relative refusal grounds are in function of protecting the private interests; they only refer to some trademarks and the competent administration does not handle them by official duty, but based on intervention by persons who have legal interest in it. This means that the sign, by itself, is not unsuitable for registration, but it is only examined and compared to previously filed or protected signs.[54]

351. Hence, LIP specifically elaborates the cases where a trademark shall not protect a sign (absolute grounds for refusal of trademark registration). The registration is refused in the cases where: the publishing or use of the sign is contrary to the public order or morality; sign which cannot be represented graphically; sign which

50. *See* LIP, Arts 219–220.
51. *See* LIP, Art. 222.
52. LIP, Art. 223.
53. *See* LIP, Art. 224.
54. Y. Reboul, Polenak Akimovska, G. Naumovski: Introduction to Trademarks and Geographical Indications, Tempus project 144582, Faculty of Law Iustinianus Primus, Skopje, 2010, p. 19–20.

is not distinctive, i.e., not capable for distinguishing goods or services in trade; sign which indicates exclusively the kind of goods or services, their purpose, time or manner of production, geographical origin, quality, price, quantity or weight; sign which has become usual in the everyday speech or in the established trade practice for marking certain type of goods, i.e., services; sign which exclusively consists of shape defined by the kind of goods, shape of goods necessary to obtain a specific technical result or shape giving a substantial value to the goods; the appearance of sign that may create confusion in trade and mislead the average consumer particularly as to the geographical origin, kind, quality or any other characteristic of the goods or services; sign that contains or consists of a geographic sign which serves to signify wines or other strong alcoholic drinks, if the reported sign refers to wines or alcoholic drinks which are not from that geographical area; sign that contains seal, official sign or hallmarks for control and guarantee of quality and imitations thereof; sign that contains a national coat of arms or other public coat of arms, flag or emblem, name or abbreviated name of a country or an international organization, as well as imitations thereof, according to Article 6-ter of the Paris Convention, except with authorization from the competent authority of the country or organization; sign that contains the name or abbreviation of that name, the coat of arms, flag, emblem or other official symbol of the Republic of Macedonia, as well as their imitations and sign that contains or imitates figure or name of a historical or dead eminent person from the Republic of Macedonia, except with authorization from the Ministry of Justice; sign that contains or imitates name, shape or other recognizable part of protected cultural inheritance of the Republic of Macedonia, except with authorization from the Administration for Protection of the Cultural Inheritance and sign that contains religious symbols or imitations thereof.[55]

352. Acquired distinctiveness is recognized in the cases where according to LIP 'the applicant proves that during the long years of use, the sign acquired distinctiveness'.[56]

353. Concerning the relative grounds for refusal, according to the LIP, a trademark may not protect a sign: which is identical to an earlier trademark filed or registered by another right-owner designating the identical kind of goods or services; which is identical to or similar to an earlier trademark, filed or registered by another right-owner designating the same or similar kind of goods or services which would create confusion at the average consumer, including the possibility of association to earlier filed for or registered trademark.[57]

354. LIP defines 'earlier filed or registered trademark' as a trademark enjoying priority right under the LIP provisions, as well as earlier internationally registered trademark with effect in the Republic of Macedonia. Furthermore, trademarks which

55. *See* LIP, Art. 176.
56. *See* LIP, Art. 177.
57. *See* LIP, Art. 178.

at the time of filing the trademark application for the sign well known in the Republic of Macedonia within the meaning of Article 6-bis of the Paris Convention or Article 16(3) from the TRIPS Agreement are also in the scope of earlier trademark.[58]

355. Also, trademark could not protect a sign which is identical or similar to an earlier registered trademark to other party, for goods, i.e., services which are neither identical nor similar to the goods, i.e., services the sign has been reported for, if the earlier registered trademark has reputation in the Republic of Macedonia and if the use of this sign, without justified reason, would represent an unfair competition or would do harm to the distinctive character or the reputation of the trademark.[59]

356. The relative grounds for refusal of trademark registration also include infringement of earlier acquired rights of: (1) the owner of a trademark registered in a country member of the Paris Union or WTO, for which the representative in the Republic of Macedonia filed an application without the owners' consent; (2) a natural right-owner whose name and surname or appearance are identical to or similar to the published sign; (3) the owner of an earlier industrial property right, if the subject matter of such right is identical to or similar to the published sign; and (4) the right-owner having copyright on the work which is identical to or similar to the published sign.[60]

357. In addition, according to LIP, trademark shall not protect a sign which is identical to or similar to a trademark, the validity of which has expired on the ground of expiring of term of protection and if the right holder failed to file a request for renewal of validity and pay the prescribed fees in the prescribed time limit, when a trademark application was filed before the expiration of the period of nine months, counting from the expiration date of the trademark validity, unless the protection of such a sign is required by the owner in whose name the trademark has been protected, or by his successor in title.[61]

§4. Formalities (Procedure for Obtaining Protection, Establishing, and Maintaining Trademarks)

358. The trademark right is acquired in a precisely formal administrative procedure released in the SOIP. The trademark application procedure begins by submitting an application to SOIP. It is essentially a one-sided procedure, and participants are the applicant and SOIP. In the appeals procedure, the one-sided procedure becomes multi-sided, as it involves stakeholders, such as the appellant.[62]

---

58. *Ibid.*
59. *See* LIP, Art. 178(4).
60. *See* LIP, Art. 178(5).
61. *See* LIP, Art. 178(6).
62. Y. Reboul, Polenak Akimovska, G. Naumovski: Introduction to Trademarks and Geographical Indications, Tempus project 144582, Faculty of Law Iustinianus Primus, Skopje, 2010, pp. 24–27.

359. The procedure for granting of a trademark right shall be initiated by filing of a trademark application to the Office. The procedure for granting of a trademark right may also be initiated by filing of an application according to the Madrid Agreement and the Madrid Protocol.[63]

360. Regarding the content of the application, it comprises the following elements: (1) request for grant of a trademark right; (2) data related to the applicant; (3) appearance of the sign for which protection is requested, and (4) list of the goods and services for which protection is requested.[64]

361. However, if the application does not contain the basic elements provided, the Office shall notify the applicant that his application is not proper, and that filing date cannot be established. If filing date of the application cannot be established, the Office shall notify the applicant to correct the deficiencies in accordance with thirty days from the date of receipt of the notification. If the applicant removes the deficiencies in the prescribed period, the Office shall determine the filing date of the Application.[65]

362. Apart from these provisions regarding the collective and certification mark, LIP also prescribes some additional registration requirements. In terms of the collective mark, LIP sets forth that the collective mark protects a sign intended for joint labelling of products or services by an organization or any other association of legal or natural persons. LIP defines any domestic organization or another association of legal and natural persons as an entity eligible for submitting a collective mark application, as well as a foreign legal person, as per the conditions set forth in LIP. The General Act or the Collective Mark Agreement is rather specific, which is submitted together with the application, and which needs to contain the following elements: company name or name of the applicant, and name of the body or person authorized to represent the applicant; provisions on the appearance of the sign and the products or services to which the sign refers; provision on who has the rights to use the collective mark and under which conditions; provision on the rights and duties of the collective mark users in case of violation of the trademark; provisions on the measures and consequences in case of a trademark violation; provisions on the measures and consequences in case of defying the provisions set forth in the General Act or Agreement.[66]

363. LIP defines the certification mark as a mark that protects a sign used by several companies under the supervision of the owner of the certification mark, and it serves for protecting the quality, origin, way of production, and other joint characteristics of the goods or services of those companies. When filing a certification mark application, the rules for using the certification mark are also enclosed, which

63. *See* LIP, Art. 180.
64. *See* LIP, Art. 181.
65. *See* LIP, Art. 182.
66. Y. Reboul, Polenak Akimovska, G. Naumovski: Introduction to Trademarks and Geographical Indications, Tempus project 144582, Faculty of Law Iustinianus Primus, Skopje, 2010, pp. 24–27.

contain provisions on the following: quality, features and other characteristics of the goods or services, control measures which the applicant for a certification mark will use and the sanctions that will apply. Pursuant to LIP, trademark protection in the Republic of Macedonia may be sought throughout the Madrid Agreement Concerning the International Registration of Marks and the Protocol Relating to the Madrid Agreement Concerning the International Registration of Marks. The protection is reversible, from the country to the Madrid Union Members and vice versa. A condition according to the Madrid Agreement, but not according to the Protocol, is a previous national registration in the country where submitter of the international application has a headquarters or residence.[67]

364. LIP affirms the concept of priority right, which appears as national and international priority right (union and convention priority right, which are minimum rights).[68] The priority right has a double meaning. First, the applicant has a priority right from the day of submitting the application in reference to all other subsequent applicants with the same or similar contents (identical or similar sign, identical or similar products or services); and second, the fulfilment of the conditions for acknowledging a right is assessed from the moment the priority right is acquired. The national priority right occurs on the day of submitting an application to SOIP. Exceptions are the union and convention priority.[69]

365. The trademark application, which application date has been established in accordance with LIP, is entered in the trademark applications register.[70]

366. The formal examination of the application is done after its entry in the applications register. The examination is in terms of whether the application contains the formal legal requirements in accordance with LIP (e.g., whether it contains all elements necessary for assessing the right for which protection is sought, whether the prescribed tax has been paid, whether evidence for the payment has been attached, whether there is a valid power of attorney in case the application was filed by a proxy).[71] If needed, SOIP calls the applicant to formally correct the application within sixty days (with a possibility for extending the deadline for additional sixty days) or on the contrary, the application is rejected with a conclusion.[72]

367. The second stage of recognizing the right to a trademark implies a material and substantive examination of the application. The presence of these components is examined from the day of submitting the application, as a day from which the

67. Y. Reboul, Polenak Akimovska, G. Naumovski: Introduction to Trademarks and Geographical Indications, Tempus project 144582, Faculty of Law Iustinianus Primus, Skopje, 2010, pp. 24–27.
68. *See* LIP, Art. 187–188.
69. Furthermore, Y. Reboul, Polenak Akimovska, G. Naumovski: Introduction to Trademarks and Geographical Indications, Tempus project 144582, Faculty of Law Iustinianus Primus, Skopje, 2010, pp. 24–27.
70. *See* LIP, Art. 1.
71. Y. Reboul, Polenak Akimovska, G. Naumovski: Introduction to Trademarks and Geographical Indications, Tempus project 144582, Faculty of Law Iustinianus Primus, Skopje, 2010, pp. 24–27.
72. *See* LIP, Art. 192.

priority right begins. In this stage of the procedure, SOIP examines the absolute grounds for refusal (as defined in Article 177 of LIP), and if such grounds are present, SOIP rejects the application with a decision. If there are no absolute grounds for refusal present, i.e., if the trademark application is in accordance with the legal requirements and the publication fees have been paid, the application data is published in SOIP's official journal – 'Glasnik'. The application is then published on SOIP's website.[73]

368. If the filed sign contains an element which is neither distinctive nor appropriate for distinctiveness of the goods, i.e., of the services in the trade and if the inclusion of that element may cause a suspicion with regard to the scope of protection of the trademark, the Office may advise the applicant, within a reasonable time limit, to submit a written statement that he does not request exclusive rights to that element. The term upon an explained request from the applicant may be extended to six months.[74]

369. Regarding the filing of opposition as significant instrument provided in LIP, it makes the procedure for recognizing the trademark right more objective, simpler, and faster. The opposition enables faster and more efficient protection of the owner and his violated rights in a special opposition procedure, during the trademark registration procedure.

370. In other words, SOIP does not pay attention to the relative grounds for refusal ex officio, but the actively identified persons may also act upon them within ninety days of the publication of the application. The opposition is a legal protection means which is filed against a trademark indicated in the published trademark application. It is a suspending legal means, as it postpones the recognition of the trademark registration. It is a two-sided legal means because the complaint is submitted to the complainant and the applicant, but it is also an autonomous legal means, as it is decided upon independently from the other trademark protection means.

371. The opposition filing deadline is within ninety days from publishing the application in the official journal of the Office. The deadline is preclusive. It may not be extended. A separate opposition filing is submitted for each application. Parties in the opposition procedure are the complainant and the applicant. LIP pays special attention to the complaint and especially the procedural presumptions that need to be fulfilled for the trademark application opposition to be taken into meritorious consideration. This will happen if the opposition is allowed, timely and complete. The opposition is allowed if filed by an eligible person – identification document for filing according to IPL. The opposition is timely if filed within the deadline

73. Y. Reboul, Polenak Akimovska, G. Naumovski: Introduction to Trademarks and Geographical Indications, Tempus project 144582, Faculty of Law Iustinianus Primus, Skopje, 2010, p. 24–27.
74. *See* LIP, Art. 194(3).

period. The opposition is complete if one can establish for which published trademark application it refers to, as well as other documentation. If the previously mentioned conditions are not met, if the opposition is not suitable for meritorious decision-making upon his grounding, SOIP rejects it with a conclusion.[75]

372. On the other hand, since as noted above, the opposition procedure is two sided, i.e., if all conditions are fulfilled (allowed, timely and complete), SOIP notifies the applicant of the reasons listed in the opposition and invites him to provide clarifications within sixty days. If the applicant does not submit the classifications of the grounds listed in the opposition, it is considered that he has no objections to the opposition filing, in which case SOIP decides upon the items in the complaint. What is the final SOIP decision? If SOIP determines that the opposition is groundless, it shall reject it with a decision. If SOIP determines that the opposition is grounded, it shall reject the trademark application, for which it submits a decision to both the applicant and the party that has filed the opposition.[76]

373. Pursuant to LIP, the trademark right is based on registration and is acquired by bringing a decision for recognizing the right (after all expenses are paid) and by recording the trademark in the trademark register kept in SOIP. The date of recording the trademark in the trademark register is identical to the date of the decision for recognizing the trademark.

§5. Ownership and Transfer (Assignment – Licences)

374. The holder of the trademark right is national and foreign legal and natural persons. Concerning foreign legal and natural persons, they enjoy the same rights as the national legal and natural persons, with regard to the protection of the industrial property rights in the Republic of Macedonia, provided that this arises from the international agreements and conventions or from the application of the principle of reciprocity. Trademark owners are also entitled to other rights provided in the provisions of international agreements and conventions, other laws, general acts, and contracts.[77]

375. Concerning trademark assignment, the assignment agreement must be composed in writing and the signatures of the contracting parties certified by notary public. Also, the agreement on request of one contracting party shall be registered in an appropriate SOIP register. The agreement on assignment of right not registered in the appropriate register of the Office shall not provide legal effect against third parties. Collective and certification marks cannot be assigned.[78]

75. *See* LIP, Art. 197–199.
76. *See* LIP, Art. 198–200.
77. *See* LIP, Arts 5–6.
78. *See* LIP, Arts 272, 222.

376. As far as licence agreements are concerned, the licence agreement must be composed in writing, i.e., the licence agreement which is not composed in writing shall not provide legal effect. The licence agreement on request of one of the contracting parties shall be registered in an appropriate register kept in the Office. The licence agreement not registered in the appropriate register of the Office shall not provide effect against third parties. The rights arising from a collective mark cannot be subject matter of the licence.[79]

377. LIP refers to the Law on Obligations concerning its application on both the assignment and licence agreements.[80]

378. The Law on Obligations also contains provisions that stipulate that if a manufacturing licence is assigned together with a licence concerning the use of a trademark, the licensee shall be entitled to put goods with such trademark on the market only if its quality is the same as the quality of goods otherwise manufactured by the licensor. A licensee shall be bound to put an indication on the goods that they are manufactured according to a licence.[81]

§6. Scope of Exclusive Rights

379. The exclusive right of the trademark holder includes the right of use, availability, right to compensation and right to forbid unlawful use by third parties.[82] Specifically, the trademark owner is entitled to the following exclusive rights:

- to use the trademark on the market for marking his goods or services.
- to use the symbol ® next to his trademark.
- to prohibit use on the market by a third right-owner, without his consent, of a sign which is: (1) identical to trademark used for identical goods or services; (2) identical to or similar to trademark used for identical or similar goods or services if that similarity may create confusion at the average consumer, including the possibility of association between the sign and the trademark; (3) identical to or similar to trademark used for different goods or services if the trademark has the reputation in the Republic of Macedonia and if the use of that sign without justified reason may lead to unfair competition and damage the distinctive character or reputation of the trademark.[83]

380. The prohibition referring to third parties also includes: (1) affixing the sign on goods and their packages; (2) rendering services or putting on the market goods

79. *Ibid.*
80. *See* LIP, Art. 274.
81. *See* LO, Arts 755–766.
82. *See* LIP, Art. 9.
83. *See* LIP, Art. 206.

under that sign, or storing goods with that intention; (3) import or export of goods under that sign; (4) use of the sign in correspondence, publishing or advertising.[84]

381. A regulation concerning reproduction of trademark in publications is also relevant for the scope of exclusive rights. Namely, in case if the reproduction of a registered trademark in dictionaries, encyclopaedia or similar publications creates an impression that it is a generic name of the products or services for which the trademark was registered, the editor of the publication shall, on request of the trademark-owner, accompany the reproduction of the trademark in the first following edition of the publication by an indication that the trademark has been registered.[85]

§7. Limitations of the Scope of Trademark Protection

382. LIP elaborates the limitations of the scope of trademark protection. The trademark owner is not entitled to prohibit third right-owners from using in trade their name, surname, sign or trade name, address, indications on the kind, quality, quantity, purpose, value, geographical origin, date of production of the goods or rendering of the services or any other characteristic of the goods, irrespective of the fact that those indications are identical to or similar to the trademark or parts thereof, provided that they are used in compliance with the good business practices and does not lead to unfair market competition.[86]

383. Furthermore, the trademark owner cannot prohibit third right-owners from using in trade a sign which is identical to or similar to a trademark if that is necessary for indicating the purpose of the goods, particularly the spare parts thereof, or the kind of services rendered if the sign is used in compliance with the good trade practices and does not lead to unfair competition.[87]

384. Regarding the doctrine of exhaustion of rights, LIP stipulates that the owner of trademark shall not have the right to prohibit use of the trademark for marking goods or services put on the domestic market by himself or with his consent, unless there have been essential changes in the goods, deterioration of their characteristics or change of the nature of the goods or services after their putting on the market.[88]

84. *Ibid.*
85. *See* LIP, Art. 209.
86. *See* LIP, Art. 207.
87. *Ibid.*
88. *See* LIP, Art. 209.

§8. Use Requirements

385. LIP clearly elaborates the use requirements. In order to maintain the trademark validity, the trademark owner should use the trademark in respect to the goods or services for which it has been granted, unless there are serious reasons for its non-use that do not depend on the trademark-owner's will. The use of a trademark in an insignificantly modified form without changing its distinctive character and the use of a trademark on goods and equipment exclusively for the purpose of export shall also constitute the use thereof. The use of a trademark by another right-owner with the owner's consent is considered to be the use by the owner himself.[89]

§9. Duration of Protection – Renewal – Termination

386. A trademark protection duration is ten years as from the date of filing the trademark application.

387. A trademark may be renewed an indefinite number of times for a term of ten years, provided that the trademark applicant files with the Office a request for renewal of the trademark validity and pays the corresponding fee and procedural expenses during the last year of the ten-year term of protection or no later than nine months after the expiration of the validity. The new period of protection shall begin with the day of expiration of the previous ten-year period of protection. In case when the application for renewal of the validity of the trademark covers only part of the goods, i.e., services for which the trademark has been registered, the validity of the trademark is renewed only for those goods, i.e., services.[90]

388. Concerning the termination of the trademark right, it emerges in one of the following cases: (1) the holder of the right without any justified reasons fails to use the trademark for marking the products, i.e., services which it refers to more than five years in continuity from the date when the trademark has been entered in the register of trademarks, i.e., from the date when the trademark has been used for the last time; (2) because of inactivity of the holder of the right it has become a usual name in the trade of the products, i.e., of the services for which it has been registered; (3) because of the method of usage by the holder of the right or by his approval, of the goods and services for which it has been registered, and which may lead the public to confusion with regard to the type, quality or the geographical origin of those goods or services, and (4) when a collective trademark is used contrary to the common act or agreement on a collective trademark.[91]

89. *See* LIP, Art. 212.
90. *See* LIP, Art. 201.
91. *See* LIP, Art. 213(1).

389. The Rulebook on Trademark defines the contents of a request for termination due to justification of the reasons for failure of the use for more than five years (described above).[92]

390. The termination procedure following the request for termination of the trademark validity is initiated upon the request of interested parties, submitted in writing to SOIP. The Office is bound, within fifteen days following the date of receipt of the request, to forward the request to the holder of the right and advise him to come out with an explanation within a determined period which cannot be longer than sixty days of the date of receipt of the notification.[93]

391. After the competition of the termination procedure, SOIP adopts a decision for termination of the validity of the trademark, or for refusal of the request for termination. The termination is into effect on the date of the validity of the termination decision adopted by SOIP. The termination decision is entered in the register of trademarks and published in the official newsletter of the Office.[94]

392. LIP also prescribes certain specificities of the procedure for trademark termination due to non-use. In this sense, if such procedure is launched, i.e., a request is submitted, the owner of the trademark is bound to prove that he does use the trademark. On the other hand, a decision for termination of the trademark due to non-use will not be enacted in the cases where the use of the trademark has started or continued after expiration of the five-year period in which it has not been used, but prior to the submission of the request for trademark termination due to non-use, unless the use has started and continued in a period of three months prior to the submission of the request for trademark termination, once the owner of the trademark has been informed that a request for trademark termination is to be submitted.[95]

393. Other reasons for termination of the validity of the trademark also include the cases where: (1) the term of protection expires and the trademark-owner fails to file, within a prescribed time limit, a request for renewal of the trademark validity and pay the prescribed fee; (2) upon a written declaration of the right-owner on waiver of the trademark, on the day following the day of filing the declaration to SOIP; (3) with the lapse of the legal right-owner or upon the death of the natural right-owner who is trademark-owner, on the day of lapse or death, or with the declaration of a missing trademark-owner dead, on the day of the coming into force of the declaration, unless the right has been transferred to the legal successors in title of the legal right-owner or to the heirs of the natural right-owner; and (4) on the basis of a court decision or act of SOIP in cases provided for by this Law, from the date prescribed in that decision or act.[96]

---

92. *See* LIP, Art. 213(2).
93. *See* LIP, Art. 214.
94. *See* LIP, Art. 215.
95. *See* LIP, Art. 276.
96. *See* LIP, Art. 217.

394. As it is the case with other industrial property rights, the decision for recognizing the trademark right may be announced void permanently during the time of protection ex officio or if proposed by the party concerned. However, if the proposal for announcing void decision for recognizing the right of trademark may not be submitted by a holder of the earlier registered trademark, if during five subsequent years prior to submitting the proposal, he was aware of the utilization of the later trademark. The proposal for announcing a decision as void shall be submitted to the Office in writing. The person submitting the request should submit all the evidence required. SOIP is bound within fifteen days upon receipt of the proposal to submit the proposal to the holder of the right and invite him to provide an opinion within sixty days from the date of receiving the notice at the latest. The decision announcing as void the decision for recognizing the trademark right shall be registered in the appropriate register and published in the official newsletter of the Office.[97]

§10. Infringement and Remedies

395. Trademark rights infringement results in civil remedies and/or criminal sanctions. Furthermore, administrative law protection is provided through the supervision provided by the competent state organ as well as through the rules of the misdemeanour procedure.

396. Concerning the civil remedies, any unauthorized use, availability, restriction, imitation, association, rights harassment, and the like contrary to the provisions of LIP is considered as infringement of the right.

397. LIP contains a specific provision on the imitation, which is deemed if the average consumer of goods or services, regardless of the type of products, may notice the difference only if he pays special attention, or if the trademark is for the translation or transcript, i.e., transliteration.[98]

398. The civil action for trademark infringement can be launched by: the person who has submitted the application for acquisition of the trademark right; the holder of the trademark right; the licensee of the exclusive licence, in scope in which he acquired the right to use, on the basis of a legal matter or law; or the authorized user of collective and certification mark.[99]

399. The civil action for trademark infringement may be filed within the deadline of three years from the date when the plaintiff became aware of the infringement and the offender, however not later than five years from the date of the infringement.[100]

97. *See* LIP, Art. 276.
98. *See* LIP, Art. 291(3).
99. *See* LIP, Art. 292.
100. *See* LIP, Art. 295.

400. Regarding the content of the action, the person whose right is infringed may demand from the court: (1) to determine if there is violation of the right; (2) to ban the actions set in the lawsuit that are violating the right; (3) to claim reimbursement occurred by the infringement of rights intentionally or by negligence; (4) to confiscate or destroy the products produced or in circulation by violation of the right and assets used for their production; (5) the defendant to provide information about the identity of third parties involved in production and distribution of goods or services infringing the rights, as well as about their distribution channels; (6) to submit the documentation and the data of the person infringing the right; (7) civil punishment; (8) publication of the verdict on the expense of the defendant; and (9) other requirements.[101]

401. The court may terminate the procedure due to trademark infringement until a decision for recognizing the appropriate right is adopted by SOIP.[102]

402. The trademark right infringer is responsible for the loss according to the general rules for compensation of damages of the Law on Obligations.[103]

403. A civil action can also be launched by a legal or natural person who can ask the court to establish whether the sign used in circulation for marking the goods or services is identical or similar to the trademark used by other legal or natural person for marking their goods or services of the same or similar kind and that this sign was well known within the meaning of Article 6 bis of the Paris Convention as a sign of the goods or services of the plaintiff before the defendant submits the trademark application. The deadline for such action is five years from the date of registration of the trademark in the trademark register. This action, however, will be rejected if the defendant or the holder of the trademark proves that before the submission of the application, he had used the disputable sign for the same or similar kind of goods or services for the same or longer period than the plaintiff.[104]

404. Furthermore, a plaintiff may claim the court to pronounce him a holder of trademark.[105]

405. Other cases of disputing the trademark right are also regulated by LIP. Hence, the person who during the time of filing the application for recognition of the right to trademark or company, i.e., name identical to the trademark of another person, may dispute this trademark for the same or similar kind of goods or services unless the holder of the trademark who was aware at the time the application was submitted, had the same company or name.[106]

101. *See* LIP, Art. 294.
102. *See* LIP, Art. 297.
103. *See* LIP, Art. 299.
104. *See* LIP, Art. 308.
105. *Ibid.*
106. *See* LIP, Art. 309.

406. Civil penalty is also prescribed in LIP, in the cases of infringement, no matter if done intentionally or with ultimate negligence. In other words, the holder of the right may ask for payment of the regular compensation increased to 200%, irrespective if due to the violation he has suffered property loss to this amount. When deciding upon the request for paying the civil penalty, and estimation of its amount, the court takes into consideration all the circumstances of the case especially the level of guilt of the defendant, the amount, the regular reimbursement as well as the preventive aim of the penalty. If the property loss is higher than the punishment, the holder of the right shall be entitled to demand the difference up to full reimbursement.[107]

407. Regarding the interim measures, the court can order them when they are proposed by the plaintiff if he provides evidence that will prove that his right has been violated or will be violated. The measures may include banning all actions of violation and their continuation; confiscation, removal from circulation and keeping of samples, means, equipment and related documents; and adoption of other similar measures. In addition to the interim measures, the court may set as a guarantee the confiscation of movable and immovable assets owned by the defendant and assets that are not directly related to the violation, as well as a ban for availability of finances on the accounts within the financial institutions and availability of other property. The courts determine the time period of this measure within the decision for interim measure. In case the measure is determined prior to the submitting of the lawsuit, the time limit within which the one proposing the guarantee must submit a lawsuit for proving the justification of these measures may not be longer than twenty days following the date of submitting the decision to the one proposing it.[108] The provisions of the Law on Securement of Claims are applied regarding the interim measures procedure.[109] LIP also stipulates measures to provide evidence such as: preparation of a detailed description of the goods proving that it has violated a specific right with or without taking a sample; confiscation of the goods which is believed that violates a specific right; confiscation of materials and means used for preparation and distribution of goods believed that violate a specific right, as well as related documentation.[110] The rules of the Law on Litigation Procedure[111] are also applied regarding the securement of evidence.[112]

408. Concerning the publishing of the judgment, the court decides on the media where it will be published as well as whether to publish the judgment fully or partially. In case if the court decides to announce only part of the judgment, then at least the purview shall be published and, if necessary, the part of the verdict showing clearly the type of the infringement and the person that has committed the infringement.[113] On the consequences of the judgment is the change in the register,

107. *See* LIP, Art. 303.
108. *See* LIP, Art. 313.
109. Official Journal of the Republic of Macedonia No. 87/07.
110. *See* LIP, Art. 314.
111. Official Journal of the Republic of Macedonia, 07/11.
112. *See* LIP, Art. 315.
113. *See* LIP, Art. 304.

done upon a request by the plaintiff, within ninety days of the date of submitting the legally effective judgment accepting the lawsuit, i.e., the registration of the plaintiff as a holder of appropriate the right as well as the issuance of the appropriate document by SOIP. Failure to submit such a request by the plaintiff results in deletion of the recognized right from the relevant register.[114]

409. Border measures for counterfeited trademarks are also part of the Macedonian legislation, in the framework of implementation of Article 51 of the TRIPS Agreement. In this context, the Law on Customs Measures for the Protection of Intellectual Property Rights (LCM)[115] entitles trademark right holders or their authorized representatives to request customs action to implement the protection of the trademark right in the cases of infringement,[116] providing the customs administration information, data and proof needed to enable the goods in question to be readily recognized by the customs authorities.[117]

410. If the request is approved, the central customs administration determines a deadline for the customs organs to act on the request.[118] Upon the approval of the request, the customs organ can suspend the release of the merchandise or detent the goods suspected of infringing an intellectual property right. Before suspending the release of or detaining the goods, the customs authority may ask the right holder to provide them with any relevant information with respect to the goods.[119] Such suspension or detention may also be conducted 'ex officio' even for goods not covered with the request of the right holder (except in the case of perishable goods).[120]

411. The customs authority provides the right holder and the declarant, the holder of the goods or the person who is the owner of the goods the opportunity to inspect the goods whose release has been suspended or which have been detained.[121] The right holder within ten working days of the receipt of notification of suspension of release or detention of the goods is bound to inform the customs authority if the goods have infringed the intellectual property right. Goods suspected of infringing an intellectual property right may be destroyed under customs control, when the following conditions are met (cumulative): (1) the right holder has confirmed in writing to the customs authorities that an intellectual property right has been infringed, within ten working days, or three working days in the case of perishable goods, of notification of the suspension of the release or the detention of the goods; (2) the right holder has confirmed in writing to the customs authority his agreement to the destruction of the goods within ten working days, or three working days in the case of perishable goods, of notification of the suspension of the release or the detention of the goods; and (3) the declarant, the holder of the goods

114. *Ibid.*
115. Official Journal of the Republic of Macedonia, 88/15, 154/15, 192/15, 23/16, 110/21.
116. *See* LCM, Art. 5.
117. *See* LCM, Art. 8.
118. *See* LCM, Art. 13.
119. *See* LCM Art. 19.
120. *See* LCM, Art. 20.
121. *See* LCM, Art. 21.

or the person who is the owner of the goods has confirmed in writing to the customs authority his agreement to the destruction of the goods within ten working days, or three working days in the case of perishable goods, of notification of the suspension of the release or the detention of the goods. Where the declarant or the holder of the goods has not confirmed his agreement to the destruction of the goods nor notified his opposition thereto to the customs authority, within those deadlines, the customs authority may deem the declarant or the holder of the goods to have confirmed his agreement to the destruction of those goods. The destruction of the goods shall be carried out under customs control and under the responsibility of the right holder. Samples may be taken by competent authority prior to the destruction of the goods, and they may be used for educational purposes.[122]

412. Absence of confirmation from the right holder regarding infringement or lack of his approval or destruction results in a release of the goods or termination of the detention, immediately after completion of all customs formalities. An exception of this is the situation where the customs authority has been duly notified of the initiation of proceedings before a competent court or other authority to determine infringement of the trademark right.[123]

413. The goods found to infringe trademark rights and expected to be destroyed cannot be: (1) released for free circulation, unless customs authorities, with the agreement of the right holder, decide that it is necessary in the event that the goods are to be disposed of or recycled outside of free circulation, including for awareness-raising, training and educational purposes; (2) brought out of the customs territory of the Republic of Macedonia; (3) exported; (4) re-exported; (5) placed under a suspensive procedure; or (6) placed in a free zone or free warehouse.[124]

414. (2) The customs authority may allow the goods referred to in paragraph (1) of this article to be moved under customs supervision between different places within the customs territory of the Republic of Macedonia with a view to their destruction under customs control.

415. LCM also provides a possibility for the Government of the Republic of Macedonia may adopt a decision the goods that are found to infringe intellectual property right to be handed over free of charge to the state authority, in cases of mitigating the consequences of natural disasters, as well as to the social welfare beneficiaries and to families whose total monthly income does not exceed 1.5 minimum wage, established for the last year.[125]

122. *See* LCM, Art. 26.
123. *Ibid.*
124. *See* LCM, Art. 28.
125. *See* LCM, Art. 30.

416. Regarding the criminal sanctions,[126] the CrC of Macedonia[127] prescribes sanctions in the case of violation of industrial property rights, including trademark rights. The provision refers to activities with 'intent to deceit buyers and users of services' as well as intent to deceit buyers, without authorization produces, release in trade, imports, exports, offer for sale or keeps objects being subject to protection of the rights. The sanction includes imprisonment of at least three years. The unauthorized use of trademark or unlawful inclusion of marks, designs or geographical indication owned by other right holders in a company name is also sanctioned in the CrC with a fine or imprisonment of up to three years.[128]

417. Considering the administrative law protection, LIP prescribes supervision by the State Market Inspectorate in the matters of unauthorized use or imitation of protected trademarks.[129] The measures include withdrawal of the products, equipment, means or related documentation from circulation, or appropriate measures for preventing further violation of the trademark right.[130] The inspector also informs the holder of the violated right so that he can submit a request for taking actions. The holder whose trademark right has been violated may submit a request in writing to the Inspectorate for taking actions for protecting the trademark right, providing the following with the request: (1) evidence that the relevant industrial property right is protected; (2) statement that he will be fully responsible towards the persons involved in the procedure for the purpose of action or omission by the holder of the right or if established that the goods in question do not violate the industrial property right; (3) technical description of the goods (precise and detailed); (4) value of the original goods in the Republic of Macedonia; (5) the location of goods; (6) details for the importer of the goods and (7) manufacturing country or countries.

418. In the misdemeanour cases, a fine in the amount of EUR 4,000 to 8,000 in denars (MKD) countervalue is foreseen for the legal person in the cases of violation through unauthorized use or imitation of a registered or protected trademark.[131]

§11. Overlapping and Relation to Other Intellectual Property Laws

419. The most evident relation of LIP trademark regulations to other intellectual property laws refers to the relation with the geographical indications, specifically

---

126. More on criminal law aspects of intellectual property in the Macedonian legislation in: Naumovski, G., Gruevska, A., Stefanovski, Lj. (2006) 'Krivično-pravna zaštita intelektualne svojine u Makedoniji', Pravni život, Časopis za pravnu teoriju i praksu, Kopaonička škola prirodnog prava Udruženja pravnika Srbije, 11/2006, p. 917–931;
127. *See* Criminal Code, Art. 285, Official Journal of the Republic of Macedonia Nos 37/96, 80/99, 48/01, 4/02, 16/02, 43/03, 19/04, 40/2004, 81/05, 50/06, 60/06, 373/06, 87/07, 7/08, 139/08, 114/09, 51/11-3, 51/11-79, 135/11, 185/11, 142/12, 143/12 166/12, 55/13, 82/13, 14/14, 27/14, 28/14, 41/14, 115/14, 132/14, 160/14, 199/14, 196/15, 226/15, 7/17, 170/17, 248/18.
128. *Ibid.*
129. *See* LIP, Art. 318(3).
130. *Ibid.*
131. *See* LIP, Art. 321(4).

regarding the absolute grounds for refusal of registration in the case where the trademark contains or consists of a geographic sign which serves to signify wines or other strong alcoholic drinks if the reported sign refers to wines or alcoholic drinks which are not from that geographical area.[132] Furthermore, as noted in §3, LIP refers to other situations where the sign for which a trademark application has been submitted infringes earlier acquired industrial property rights, as well as where the trademark infringes the rights of an owner that holds having copyright on the work which is identical to or similar to the published sign.[133] In this context, it is beneficial for intellectual property practitioners, including examiners, judiciary, attorneys and enforcement agencies to take into account other related laws, such as the CL,[134] as well as the Law on Quality of Agricultural Products (LQAP),[135] and Law on Wines.[136]

420. An interesting issue in Macedonian legislation is the issue of relation of trademarks to domain names, having in mind the absence of clear primary legislation for domain names and trademarks domain name disputes,[137] especially since in the Macedonian legal practice, it is possible to register a domain name as a trademark.

132. *See* LIP, Art. 177(8).
133. *See* LIP, Art. 178(5).
134. Official Journal of the Republic of Macedonia No. 115/10, 140/10, 51/11, 147/13, 154/15 и 27/16.
135. Official Journal of the Republic of Macedonia, Nos 140/10, 53/11, 55/12, 106/13, 116/15 и 149/15, 193/2015.
136. Official Journal of the Republic of Macedonia, Nos 50/10, 53/11, 53/11, 6/12, 64/12, 23/13, 106/13, 188/13, 149/15, 339/16, 172/16, 174/2016, 70/18, 235/19.
137. The rules for domain name disputes are set down in the Rulebook for Organization and administration of the top-level Macedonian.mk domain and the top-level Macedonian. mkd domain. Available at: https://marnet.mk/doc/pravilnik-mk-mkd.pdf.

Chapter 4. Trade Names

§1. Sources – Legislation

421. Provisions relevant for trade names in Macedonian law are present in the Law on Trade Companies (LTC),[138] the CrC,[139] the Law on Consumer Protection (LCP).[140] Provisions for trade name protection in ratified industrial property conventions and agreements are also part of the Macedonian legal system.

§2. Protection of Trade Names

I. Law on Trade Companies

422. Tradename can be protected as business name (in Macedonian: *firma),* under the provisions of LTC. LTC stipulates that every commercial entity in the course of the day-to-day communication in writing, in electronic or in any other way, shall be obliged in an easy, direct and constantly accessible manner to use and make available the business name.[141] The business name under which the activity is to be performed is registered in the trade register in the Central Register of the Republic of Macedonia.[142] The business name of the trade company is the name used by the company in its operations and under which it participates in the legal operation. The business name of the trade company is determined and changed in the manner determined by the act of incorporation of a company by a single person, with the company's agreement, that is the statute. The business name of the trade company and all its changes are registered in the trade register.[143]

138. Official Journal of the Republic of Macedonia Nos 28/2004, 84/2005, 25/2007, 87/2008, 42/2010, 48/2010, 24/2011, 166/2012, 70/2013, 119/2013, 120/2013, 187/2013, 38/2014, 41/2014, 138/2014, 88/2015, 192/2015 and 6/2016. Decisions of the Constitutional Court of the Republic of Macedonia U. No. 177/2005 dated 24 May 2006, published in the 'Official Journal of the Republic of Macedonia' No. 71/2006, U. No. 177/2008 dated 14 Jan. 2009, published in the 'Official Journal of the Republic of Macedonia' No. 17/2009, U. No. 153/2008 dated 11 Feb. 2009, published in the 'Official Journal of the Republic of Macedonia' No. 23/2009, U. No. 75/2010 dated 12 Jan. 2011, published in the 'Official Journal of the Republic of Macedonia' No. 8/2011, and U. No. 169/2010 dated 9 Feb. 2011, published in the 'Official Journal of the Republic of Macedonia' No. 21/2011.
139. Official Journal of the Republic of Macedonia Nos 37/96, 80/99, 4/02, 43/03, 19/04, 81/05, 60/06, 73/06, 7 /08, 139/08, 114/09, 51/11, 135/11, 55/13, 220/2000, 16/02/, 40/04, 50/06.185/2011, 142/2012, 166/2012,. 28/2004, 84/2005, 25/2007, 87/2008, 42/2010, 48/2010, 24/2011, 166/2012, 70/2013, 119/2013, 120/2013, 187/2013, 38/2014, 41/2014, 138/2014, 88/2015, 192/2015 and 6/2016.
140. Official Journal of the Republic of Macedonia Nos 38/04, 77/07, 103/08, 24/11, 164/13, 97/15, 152/15.
141. LTC, Art. 10.
142. LTC, Art. 14.
143. LTC, Art. 44.

423. Concerning the content of the business name, according to LTC, the business name contains designation referring to the scope of operation of the trade company, the head office and the type of the company.[144] The business name can contain additions (drawings, pictures, symbols, and alike used for detailed marking of the trade company), except the ones creating or that can create confusion in regard to the scope of operation of the trade company, the impression of the identity or the connection of the other trade company or if such data can violate industrial property rights or other rights of other trade companies, that is persons registered in the country and abroad.[145] LTC regulates that the business name can be also used as a trademark, in a manner and under the conditions determined by law.[146]

424. There are several restrictions regarding the content of the business name. Namely, it cannot contain names, flags, coats of arms or other state symbols of other states or international organization without their approval, nor they can be imitated in heraldic sense. Also, the business name cannot contain official signs of quality control and quality assurance. The business name cannot contain words that are misleading or that can create confusion with the business name of another company, that is name of an institution or another entity.[147]

425. According to LTC, the word 'Macedonia', and the words derived thereon, as well as its abbreviations, the flag and the coat of arms can be contained in the business name only with an approval from the Ministry of Justice. Respectively, an approval from the competent body of the local-self-government unit shall be required when the business name consists of words containing the name of the local self-government unit.[148]

426. Regarding names and surnames, a name and a surname of natural persons can be included in the business name only with his/her consent, or, if that natural person is deceased, with the consent of his/her descendants in a direct line up to a third degree. A name and surname of a historical or another famous person can be included in the business name, only with the consent of the person, or, if the person is deceased, with the consent of his/her descendants in a direct line up to the third degree and, if such consent does not exist, the consent shall be given by the Ministry of Justice. If the honour or reputation of a natural person whose full name and surname are included in the business name of a company is in any way violated, upon his/her request, and if he/she is deceased, upon a request of his/her inheritors, the court upon a lawsuit shall prohibit such usage. If within eight days as of the day of the legally valid decision for the prohibition was passed, an application for change of the business name is not submitted, the court shall appoint a liquidator that shall perform liquidation of the trade company.[149]

144. LTC, Art. 45.
145. LTC, Art. 46 (1,2).
146. LTC, Art. 46(3).
147. LTC, Art. 47.
148. LTC, Art. 48.
149. LTC, Art. 49.

427. The business name of the trade company has to be in the Macedonian language and its Cyrillic letter, while the business name of the trade company having a head office on the territory of a local-self-government unit where at least 20% of the citizens speak official language other than Macedonian can be also expressed in that language and used only together with the text in the business name in Macedonian language and its Cyrillic letter.[150]

428. If the company is in bankruptcy or liquidation, i.e., if a bankruptcy or liquidation procedure has been initiated, the business name contains a designation 'in bankruptcy' or 'in liquidation', and as is entered in the trade register.[151]

429. As far as the manner of use of the business name is concerned, the trade company, during its operation, shall have to use the business name as it is entered in the trade register. The trade company can also use an abbreviated business name that has to include a designation to distinguish the company from other trade companies, abbreviated designation of the company type with the head office. The abbreviated business name is also recorded in the trade register. The business name or the abbreviated business name shall have to be displayed on the business premises.[152]

430. It is important that the new business names in the trade companies have to be clearly distinct from the business names of companies entered in the trade register. A business name identical to a business name that has already been entered or such that does not clearly differ from an already entered business name cannot be entered in the trade register, which is inspected ex officio.[153]

431. The principle of priority is applied for the purpose of entry in the trade register. In other words, if two identical business names or business names that do not differ from one another are filed, the business name that has been filed first (first submitted business name) shall be entered into the register.[154]

432. An exception from this rule is the situation where the user of the later submitted business name has been using the business name or its main components as a mark of the enterprise or as a trademark for designation of the products or services, prior to the submission of the previously submitted (first submitted) file. In this case, the later business name will be entered in the register even if it is submitted second. In order for the registration to be realized, however, the person filing the later business name has to prove the above-mentioned use.[155]

433. LTC contains clear provisions on the protection of the rights of the owner of a previously filed business name. Namely, a commercial entity which, by using

150. LTC, Art. 50.
151. LTC, Art. 51.
152. LTC, Art. 52.
153. LTC, Art. 56.
154. LTC Art. 57(1).
155. LTC Art. 57(2).

a similar content of a business name entered in the commercial register, violates the rights of another commercial entity or endangers his/her position in the market, or there is danger that his/her rights and position in the market to be violated or endangered or the commercial entity uses his business authority or assumes it without authorization, or if the other commercial entity (by using the business name) without an authorization uses his/her business status or adopts it, he/she can file a lawsuit and prohibit the other commercial entity from using the business name, as well compensate the damage caused by using the business name. If within a time period of eight days as of the day of the legally valid decision for prohibition a file is not submitted regarding the change of the business name, the court shall appoint a liquidator that shall conduct the liquidation of the trade company. The lawsuit can be filed within a period of three years as of the day of publication of the entry of the business name. The legally valid court decision accepting the lawsuit request shall be published by the court at the expense of the defendant in a newspaper determined by the defendant.[156]

434. Notwithstanding the other regulations, LTC prescribes that the commercial entity can protect his/her intellectual property rights in regard to the use and entry of the business name in the trade register on the basis of CL and LIP.

435. LTC promulgates that transfer of a business name from one entity to another is possible only if the transfer is together with the transfer of the enterprise or with transfer of the predominant part of the enterprise. For a transfer of the business name containing name of a natural person, a consent from that person is required, or if that person is deceased, a consent from his/her relatives in a direct line up to a third-degree kinship.[157] In other cases, if a new member/partner joins the trade company or if one of the members/partners leaves the company, the existing business name can be still used.[158]

II. Criminal Code

436. The CrC promulgates the misuse of trade (business) name in the context of violation of industrial property rights. Namely, it stipulates that in the case of unauthorized use of trade names or unauthorized inclusion of trademarks, industrial designs, geographical indications and appellations of origin in the business name, a pecuniary punishment or imprisonment of up to three years could be imposed as a sanction to the perpetuator.[159] If significant property benefit or significant property damage is caused by the unauthorized use of business name, the sentence is imprisonment of one to five years plus a pecuniary punishment. If the crime is committed by an organized group or the crime has caused risk to human life and health, the

156. LTC Art. 58.
157. LTC Art. 53.
158. LTC, Art. 54.
159. Criminal Code, Art. 285.

offender shall be sentenced to imprisonment of at least five years, while if the perpetuator is a legal entity, it shall be fined. The objects made or used for committing the crime are seized in the above cases.[160]

III. Law on Consumers' Protection (LCP)

437. LCP enumerates the data that are compulsory elements regarding product declaration. In this sense, the compulsory elements of the declaration are: the name of the product, i.e., the name under which the product is sold; the composition of the product; way of maintaining the product; manner of use of the product; industrial design, trademark or marking of the product, if they are important elements of the product; date of production and expiration date, if it is prescribed; company and headquarters of the manufacturer, i.e., the merchant, if it has its own trademark for the product and is presented as a manufacturer, and for import products and company and headquarters (full address) of the importer, as well as the country of origin; warning of possible danger during use, if such danger exists; statement of the manufacturer for the existence of changed properties of the products, components of the parts and accessories, i.e., what changes are in question and statement of the manufacturer for compliance of the products with the prescribed conditions.[161]

438. LCP furthermore contains provisions on market behaviour that is considered fraudulent if it contains false information and is therefore untrue or in any way, including the general impression it leaves, deceives or is likely to deceive the consumer, and in any case causes or is likely to cause the average consumer to make a decision that he would not bring in another case. This information might refer *inter alia* to the existence or nature of the product and service, or the main features of the product and service.[162] According to LCP, the behaviour is considered fraudulent also if it misleads the consumer to make a decision regarding any marketing of a product or service, including comparative advertising, which leads to confusion with other products and services, trademarks, trade names or other characteristics by which competitors differ.[163]

---

160. *Ibid.*
161. LCP, Art. 23.
162. LCP, Art. 31-b (1).
163. LCP, Art. 31-b (2).

Chapter 5. Industrial Designs

§1. Sources – legislation

439. Industrial design is regulated in a separate part in the LIP (Articles 127–174). Other laws, such as those regulating customs procedures in relation to intellectual property rights, or judicial protection, apply as well. In addition, by-laws regulate in more detail different technical aspects. The most relevant is the Rulebook on industrial design.[164] The relevant international treaties, including The Hague Agreement, are also part of the national legal order and a source of law.

§2. Subject Matter of Protection

440. Article 127 of the LIP specifies the subject matter of protection of industrial design. The right to industrial design shall protect the design which is new and has individual character. The term 'design' is defined as the outer appearance of a product as a whole or of its part which is determined by its characteristics, in particular, the lines, contours, colours, shape, texture and the materials which the product is made of or ornamented, and/or its decorations. The 'product' can be an industrial or handcraft item, including, *inter alia*, parts intended to be combined into a complex product, packaging of the product, graphic symbols, typographical signs, except computer programs. 'Complex product' is a product composed of several parts which could be replaced so that they enable dismantling and assembling of the product again. The design applied to a product or contained in a product which composes an integral part of a complex product shall be deemed new and that it has an individual character if:

(1) the component part built in a complex product remains visible throughout the normal use of the complex product; in this context, normal use means use by the end user, excluding maintenance, servicing and repair of the product; and
(2) the visible characteristics of the component part fulfil the conditions of novelty and individual character.

§3. Conditions of Protection

441. The two conditions of protection are novelty (Article 128) and individual character of the design (Article 129). The design shall be considered as new if an identical design has not become available to the public prior to the date of filing of the application for granting of that particular design or if there has been a claim for a priority right prior to the date of the claimed priority right or if there is no earlier application filed for granting of an identical design. A design shall be also considered as identical when it differs in non-essential parts.

164. Official Journal of RNM No. 92/2009.

442. It is considered that the design has become available to the public if it had been published, exhibited, used in trade or otherwise disclosed prior to the date of filing of an application for design granting or the date of the priority right, unless the disclosure, due to justified reasons, could not have been known in the regular operation in the specialized areas in the Republic of Macedonia, prior to the date of filing of the application for an industrial design or if a priority right has been requested, prior to the date of the priority. It shall not be considered that a design has become available to the public if it has been disclosed by a third party under clear or assumed conditions of secrecy, or disclosed by the designer, his legal successor or a third party on the basis of information or activities undertaken by them in the course of twelve months, prior to the date of filing the application or the date of the priority if applicable.

443. The design shall be considered to have individual character if the total impression it makes to the informed user differs from the total impression to the same user of any other design which has become available to the public prior to the date of filing the application for granting industrial design, or if a priority right has been claimed prior to the date of the granted priority right. When assessing the individual character of a design, the degree of freedom that the author has had while creating the design shall be taken into consideration.

444. The LIP contains a negative definition as well, specifying in which cases a design cannot be protected by the right of industrial design. According to Article 131, this will be the case if:

- the design is exclusively determined by the technical functions of the product; or
- it has to be reproduced in its accurate shape and dimensions so the product in which it is contained or on which the design is applied to could be mechanically connected to another product or placed inside, near or around another product so that the two products could perform their function. However, in this case, if the conditions of novelty and individual character are fulfilled, a design which enables multiple assembling or connection of mutually replaceable products in a modular system may be protected.

445. Article 132 provides a list of absolute grounds for refusal to grant the right of industrial design. The design cannot be protected by a right of industrial design if it:

(1) is not in accordance with the definition of design under Article 127;
(2) is contrary to the public order or the morality;
(3) represents a technical plan or a scheme;
(4) represents exclusively cartographic or photographic work;
(5) contains state or other public coat of arms, flag or emblem, title or abbreviation of the title of an international organization, unless a permission has been obtained from the competent authority of the respective country or organization – for the Republic of North Macedonia it is the Ministry of Justice;

(6) contains or imitates the figure or name of a historical or deceased famous person from the Republic of North Macedonia, unless a permission has been obtained from a competent state body – for the Republic of North Macedonia, it is the Ministry of Justice;
(7) contains or imitates the name, shape or other recognizable parts of protected cultural inheritance in the Republic of North Macedonia, unless a permission has been obtained from a competent state body – for the Republic of Macedonia, it is the Cultural Inheritance Protection Authority.

446. In addition, the LIP in Article 133 lists several relative grounds for refusal, where a design may not be protected by an industrial design right if it is not new; it does not have an individual character; or it cannot be protected pursuant to Article 131.

447. An industrial design may not protect a design which infringes previously acquired rights of the holder of a previously protected right from industrial property, or of the person who has copyright in a work identical or similar to the design. These grounds could be invoked only by the applicant of a previously filed application or the holder of a previously acquired right.

448. Industrial design that has been submitted for application earlier shall be a reason for refusal only if it is registered.

§4. Formalities (Procedure for Grant and Obtaining Protection)

449. Under Article 134, the procedure for acquiring a right to industrial design may be initiated by the author or his successor only. If the design is creation of several authors, then all the authors and their successors are entitled to initiate the procedure. If the application has not been filed by the author, then it shall be deemed that it has been filed in accordance with the LIP, until proved to the contrary. Application for industrial design could also be filed by the person commissioning the design if it has been made on the basis of a commission contract, unless otherwise determined by the contract. The application may also be filed by the employer if the design is made by an employee during his working obligations, in line with the instructions of his employer, unless otherwise determined by the work contract.

450. The procedure for granting an industrial design right is initiated by filing an application for industrial design right to the Office (Article 137). The procedure may also be initiated by filing an application in accordance with The Hague Agreement. Procedure for international registration of an industrial design, in accordance with the provisions of The Hague Agreement, shall be initiated by filing an application for international registration of industrial design directly to the International Bureau of the WIPO.

451. Separate application is filed for each design for which protection is requested (Article 138). It shall be possible to request protection of more designs of products (multiple applications) through one application for granting of an industrial property right. If a multiple application is filed, all designs from the application have to be intended to be applied to products classified in the same class according to the Locarno classification. The multiple application may contain maximum a hundred designs.

452. The right of priority is regulated in Articles 139–144. From the date of receipt of the complete application for industrial design in the Office, the applicant has the right to priority in relation to any other person who files an application for the same design. An exception to this is when the conditions for filing an application for industrial design under exhibition priority right or union priority right are fulfilled.

453. A person who exhibits a design at an officially acknowledged international exhibition or fair in the Republic of Macedonia or in other Member State of the Paris Union or WTO may, within three months from the date when the exhibition (fair) is closed, apply for a right to priority from the first day of the exhibit or from the date of use. The application has to be accompanied by a written confirmation from the competent authority of the Member State of the Paris Union or the WTO confirming that it is an officially acknowledged exhibition (fair) according to the Convention on International Exhibitions and including data for the type of the exhibition or fair, the venue in which it takes place, the starting and ending date or the date of use. By acknowledging the priority right, the deadlines relating to union priority right shall not be extended.

454. A legal or a natural person that has filed a regular application for industrial design in a Member State of the Paris Union or the WTO shall be acknowledged union priority right in the Republic of Macedonia from the date of submission of its first application, if requested so within six months from the date of submission of the first application. Regular application is considered the application the date of submission of which has been established in accordance with the national legislation of the Member State of the Paris Union or the WTO in which the application has been filed, or in accordance with the international treaties signed between the Member States of the Union, regardless of the legal destiny of the application later on.

455. The applicant who intends to use the union priority right shall be obliged, in the application filed in the Republic of Macedonia, to state all data concerning the application he invokes, and within three months from the date of submission of the application for acknowledgement of the priority right, to submit a copy of the first application, certified by the competent authority of the Member State of the Paris Union or the WTO in which the application has been filed.

456. The applicant for industrial design may invoke the multiple priority right on the basis of several previously filed applications in one or more Member States of the Paris Union or the WTO. If the applicant invokes the multiple priority right, the deadlines which start with the date of the granted priority right shall be counted from the earliest date of the multiple priority right.

457. At the request of the applicant, the Office shall issue a certificate on priority right which is valid from the date established as date of filing the application for industrial design.

458. Under Article 145, the application for industrial design must contain the following elements:

(1) request for granting of the right to industrial design;
(2) data related to the applicant;
(3) representation of the design for which protection is requested.

459. The application can be accompanied by other elements and attachments. If a request to postpone the publication of an application for a two-dimensional industrial design according to Article 155 paragraph (1) has been filed, the request may also be accompanied by samples of the product on which the design has been applied instead of summaries of the design.

460. If the application does not contain the required elements, the Office shall notify the submitter that their application is not complete and the date of submission cannot be recognized (Article 146). The Office shall invite the applicant within thirty days from the receipt of the invitation to remove the shortcomings. If the submitter eliminates the shortcomings, the Office shall determine the application submission date. The date on which the applicant corrected the shortcomings and acted in line with the notification shall be regarded as application date. If the submitter fails to eliminate the shortcomings, it shall be considered that the application is withdrawn, and the procedure shall be stopped. The application is entered into the register for industrial design applications (Article 147).

461. At the request of the applicant, a multiple application for industrial design may be divided into two or more applications in the course of the procedure for granting of the right to industrial design (Article 148). Division of an application is possible until adoption of the decision to grant the industrial design right. Such application created by division of the multiple application shall keep the filing date of the first application and shall also keep the priority right if there is a claim for it.

462. Pursuant to Article 149, an application for industrial design shall be duly complete if:

(1) it includes all the necessary parts and enclosures provided for in Article 145 and in by-laws;
(2) a power of attorney is enclosed, when the application is filed through an agent;
(3) a translation of the application into Macedonian language is submitted if the application is written in a foreign language;

(4) the application tax is paid and an evidence for the payment is submitted.

463. Following the registration of the application in the register of applications, the Office shall examine if the application is complete (Article 150). If the Office finds that the application is not complete, it shall invite the applicant to correct the shortcomings within a deadline no longer than sixty days, from the date of receiving the notification. At the elaborated request of the applicant, the deadline may be extended for maximum sixty days. If the applicant fails to correct the shortcomings, the Office shall reject the application. When the applicant invokes attachments which are not included in the application, the Office shall invite the applicant to submit them within the set deadline. If the applicant does not proceed according to the notification, it shall be deemed that such attachments do not exist. If the applicant corrects the application within the specified deadline, it shall be considered that the application is duly filed.

464. After the formal examination, if the application is complete, the Office shall examine whether the conditions for granting of the industrial design right are fulfilled (Article 151).

465. If the industrial design may not be granted due to reasons referred to in Article 132, the Office shall take a decision for total or partial rejection of the application (Article 152). The Office may not take such a decision if it has not previously informed the applicant in writing about the reasons for which the right could not be granted as a whole or in the requested scope, and if it has not invited the applicant to respond within a reasonable time limit, which may, at an elaborated request by the applicant, be extended up to six months. When responding, the applicant may not additionally change the design.

466. If the application fulfils the formal requirements of Article 149, and if the design has not been excluded from protection according to Article 132, the Office shall invite the applicant to pay, within a time limit no longer than thirty days, the costs for publication of the application data in the Official Journal of the Office (Article 153). If the applicant fails to pay, the Office shall reject the application. If the applicant pays the expenses, the Office shall publish the application data in the Official Journal of the Office within ninety days at the latest (Article 154).

467. The applicant for an industrial design may, at the same time with submission of the application, ask for postponement of the publication for a period of twelve months, counted from the date of filing the application or, if priority right has been claimed, from the date of the priority right (Article 155). If postponement is requested, the Office shall publish application data in the official journal, in a way established by a regulation adopted by the director of the Office. In the case of postponement, upon the expiration of the time limit for postponement of the publication or of any other previous date that the applicant has stated in the application, the Office shall invite the applicant to submit, within thirty days, photographs and graphic drawings of the design as stated in the application, in compliance with

Article 145 paragraph (1) item 3 and pay the costs referred to in Article 153 paragraph (1). If the applicant fails to proceed in accordance with the notification, the application shall be rejected. In case of multiple applications, these provisions can be applied to any of the designs included in such an application.

468. Articles 156–158 specify details about objection to the application for industrial design. An objection to the published application for industrial design could be lodged to the Office, within ninety days from the date of publication, by:

(1) an applicant of previously registered industrial design and holder of previously granted industrial design right;
(2) holder of previously acquired industrial property right, if the subject of that right is identical or similar to the published industrial design;
(3) person who has copyright to a work identical or similar to the published industrial design; and
(4) an interested person who believes that the published industrial design is not in compliance with the requirements for novelty and individual character or that it is exclusively limited to the functional characteristics of the product.

469. A separate objection shall be lodged for each published application for industrial design.

470. The Office shall examine whether an objection has been lodged by a person entitled to lodge objection and within the prescribed deadline. If these requirements are not fulfilled, the Office shall reject the objection. If the requirements are fulfilled, the Office, within a period of fifteen days following the receipt, shall submit the objection to the applicant for industrial design and invite him to respond to the reasons stated in the objection, within a period not longer than sixty days. If the applicant does not respond, the Office shall decide on the basis of the claims in the objection.

471. If the applicant submits a reply to the objection, the Office shall examine the justification for the objection, taking into consideration the reasons for the objection and the reply. If the Office finds that there is no ground for the objection, it shall reject the objection by a decision forwarded to both the applicant and the person who lodged the objection. If the Office finds that the objection is founded, it shall take a decision to reject the application and shall forward it to both the applicant and the person who lodged the objection.

472. If there is no objection lodged within a defined period or if the objection is rejected, the Office shall notify the applicant, within thirty days following the date of the receipt of the notification, to pay the maintenance fee for the first five years of the validity of the industrial design, the costs for the publication in the Official Journal of the Office, and the costs for issuance of a certificate for industrial design

(Article 159). If the applicant pays the fees and costs, the Office shall issue a decision granting the right of industrial design and shall enter the granted right in the register for industrial designs. If the applicant does not pay within the deadline, the Office shall reject the application.

473. The changes related to the applicant, the holder of the right and the right itself are entered in the register of applications for industrial design and in the register of industrial designs (Article 160). The changes entered in the register of applications for industrial design after publication of an application and the changes filed in the register of industrial designs shall be published in the Official Journal of the Office.

474. The scope of protection of the industrial design is determined by the characteristics of the design given in the presentation and the characteristics supported in the description if available (Article 161). Protection arising from the industrial design right shall cover the design in the scope in which it does not make a different overall impression to the informed customer. When assessing the scope of protection, the freedom the designer had in the course of creation of the design shall be taken into consideration.

475. Industrial design right shall be acquired on the date of adopting the decision to grant the right and with the entry in the register, both of which need to be on the same date (Article 162). The data on the industrial design shall be published in the Official Journal of the Office, within ninety days from the date of entering the industrial design in the register (Article 163). The Office shall issue a certificate to the holder of the industrial design within six months following the date of the decision to grant the right of industrial design (Article 164).

§5. Ownership and Transfer (Assignment – Licences)

476. The author is a natural person who has created the design by his creative labour (Article 135). The person who in the creation of the design has offered technical assistance only shall not be deemed as author. Legal successor of the author, as a right holder, shall be a legal or natural person whose acquirement of the right to industrial design is based on law, legal deed, inheritance or court decision (Article 136).

477. According to Article 271 of the LIP, the industrial design right applicant and the holder of the right may transfer his right in its entirety or in part, by agreement, in accordance with the applicable laws. The transfer agreement must be composed in writing and the signatures of the contracting parties must be certified by notary public; otherwise, it shall not produce any legal effect. At the request of any contracting party, the agreement is registered in the register kept in the Office; otherwise, it shall not produce legal effect against third parties.

478. The LIP contains provisions on a licence agreement in Article 272. The applicant and the holder of the right may assign that right for use by licence agreement, in accordance with the LIP or other regulations. The licence agreement must be composed in writing; otherwise, it does not produce any legal effect. If several persons have submitted an industrial design application or if the right holders are several entities, the consent of all these persons shall be necessary for concluding the licence agreement. If there is no consent, the rules of co-ownership apply to the assigning of the right to usage. At the request of one of the contracting parties, the licence agreement shall be registered in the register kept in the Office. If it is not registered, it shall not have effect against third parties.

479. According to Article 273, a provision of the licence agreement shall be void if it sets limitations to the licence user which do not result from the right that is subject to the agreement or if it is not necessary for keeping that right, or if it is contrary to the regulations relating to competition.

480. In addition to these specific provisions on the transfer of rights in the LIP, the Law on Obligations as a *lex generalis* applies to the agreements for transfer and licence, as stipulated in Article 274.

§6. Scope of Exclusive Rights

481. As industrial design has a creative dimension, the author enjoys moral rights in addition to exploitation rights. According to Article 165, the author, regardless of whether he is applicant or holder of the right, shall always have the moral right to be stated as author of the industrial design in all documents and public materials. The moral right is not transferable. If the design has been created by several authors, they all have equal rights, regardless of the contribution in the creation of the industrial design, and as a consequence all of them have to be stated as authors.

482. A holder of an industrial design shall have the exclusive right to use the industrial design and prevent third parties from using it without his consent, under Article 166. Usage shall cover, in particular, manufacture, supply, putting into circulation, export, import or usage of the product in which the design is contained or to which the design has been applied, or storage of such products for certain purposes. If the publication of an industrial design is postponed according to Article 155, during the period of postponement, the holder shall have the right to prevent third parties from use in case when it is the result of the copying of the industrial design.

§7. Limitations of the Scope of Protection

483. Pursuant to Article 167, it shall not be considered as infringement of the exclusive rights of the holder of the industrial design if products made according to the industrial design are used in construction or in ship equipment, air planes or land vehicles belonging to a Member State of the Paris Union or WTO, when such means of transportation are found, temporarily or by chance, in the territory of the Republic of North Macedonia, provided that the built-in product serves exclusively to the needs of these means of transportation.

484. The exclusive rights of use shall not apply to the usage of an industrial design for:

(1) private and non-commercial purposes;
(2) informing the public or for the purpose of education, if it is in accordance with the good business practices and if it does not harm the interests of the holder of the right and of the author;
(3) experimental and scientific purposes.

485. In addition, the right holder may not invoke the exclusive rights against a third party that has used the same design of the product or made all preparations for use of the same design of a product prior to the date of filing the application to the Office or prior to the acquired priority right, provided that the third party has made the product without having any information about the existence of the industrial design which at that time was not available to the public. A third party may not use the design in a manner that goes beyond the limits of regular production activities. A person who has the right on the basis of previous use may not give a licence to a third party to use the design. The right to prior usage is not transferable, unless the right of transfer is transferred together with the enterprise or the workshop where the use of such a design was prepared or started.

486. Article 170 stipulates that the holder of the previously granted industrial design has no right to ask for cancellation of a subsequently granted industrial design on the basis of his priority right, nor to forbid use of the subsequently granted same or similar industrial design, if he has knowingly tolerated such a usage in a period of five years, unless the subsequently granted industrial design has been protected negligently. The holder of a subsequently granted industrial design has no right to forbid the holder of the previously granted industrial design from using it.

487. Article 171 covers the principle of exhaustion. The holder of the industrial design right shall have no right to prohibit the sale of products to which the design has been applied if he himself has placed them on the domestic market or they are placed on the market with his approval, unless there has been a change in the character of the design.

§8. Duration of Protection

488. The industrial design shall be valid for a period of five years, starting from the date of filing the application (Article 172). The validity may be extended several times for a period of five years, but not more than twenty-five years. The holder of the industrial design submits a request to extend the validity during the last year of validity of the protection and shall enclose proof for the payment of the fee and costs of the procedure for extension. Request for extension may also be filed within six months after the expiry of the validity, by payment of additional filing fee. The new term of protection shall start to run on the date following the date of expiry of the previous period of validity, and it shall be entered in the register and published in the official journal of the Office.

489. Article 173 governs the termination of the validity of the design. The industrial design right shall cease to be valid in the following cases:

(1) if the term of validity has passed;
(2) on the basis of a written statement by the right holder stating that he waives the right to industrial design, on the day following the date the statement is submitted to the Office; and
(3) if the legal person which is a holder of the industrial design right has ceased to operate – starting on the date of cessation, or if the natural person who is a holder of the right has died – starting with the date of his death, or if a disappeared person who is a holder of the right has been pronounced dead – starting on the date when the decision takes effect, unless this right has been assigned to the legal successors. The termination of the validity of the industrial design right shall be entered in the register on industrial designs.

490. According to Article 174, if a licence, pledge or some other right has been filed in the register for industrial design in favour of a third party, the holder of the industrial design may not waive his rights without prior written consent from the third party. If the holder of an industrial design does not pay the fee within a prescribed period, and a licence, pledge or some other right has been entered in the register in favour of a third party, the Office shall notify that person that the fee has not been paid, and he may pay it within a six-month period, starting from the date of notification, in order to maintain the registered right. In case of a dispute for securing the registered rights of a third party, the court may, if necessary to secure those rights, decide to assign the industrial design right to the person on whose behalf the licence, pledge or other right has been registered, until the claims are settled.

§9. Infringement and Remedies

491. The rules regarding judicial protection for infringement of the industrial design right are covered in Part X of the LIP and apply to all the rights covered within the scope of the Law. As a general rule, according to Article 291, the person whose right is infringed is entitled to protection of the right by submitting a lawsuit to the court with competence to settle disputes regarding industrial property rights. Infringement of the registered and recognized rights is any unauthorized use, disposal, limitation, imitation, association, rights disturbance and the like, contrary to the provisions of the Law. Imitation occurs if the average consumer of goods or services, regardless of the type of products, may notice the difference only if he pays special attention.

492. The following persons are entitled, according to Article 292, to initiate a lawsuit relating to right protection:

- the submitter of the application for protection of right;
- the holder of the right;
- the licensee of the exclusive licence, in scope in which he acquired the right to use, on the basis of a legal deed or law;

493. When a right is infringed, each of the holders of that right may in respect of any third party demand protection of the right as if he was a single holder. When a person infringing the right fulfils the requirements to one of the holders of the right, its obligation towards the other holders of the right shall cease. In case of ongoing legal proceedings, the holders of the same right shall be deemed as a single party in the litigation.

494. The content of the lawsuit is specified in Article 294. The person whose right is infringed may demand from the court:

(1) to determine the infringement of the right;
(2) to ban the actions set in the lawsuit that are infringing the right;
(3) to claim compensation for damages caused by infringement of rights intentionally or by negligence. The rules on obligations apply in such cases.
(4) to confiscate or destroy the products produced or in circulation by infringement of the right and means used for their production. The court applies the principle of proportionality when considering this claim.
(5) to order the defendant to provide information about the identity of third parties involved in production and distribution of goods or services infringing the rights, as well as about their distribution channels;
(6) to submit the documentation and the data about the person infringing the right;
(7) civil penalty, in case of intention or gross negligence;
(8) publication of the judgment at the expense of the defendant; and
(9) other claims. In the case of industrial designs, the author, his successor or other legal successor may request from the court during the validity period to declare him as the holder of the industrial design if the design right is issued under the name of a person who is not the author, his successor or other legal successor. The author of the design may also request to be specified in the application and all the other documents, and following his death, this claim can be made by his successors. In this case, the lawsuit may be initiated from the date of filing the application form as well as during the whole time of validity of the industrial design.

495. The lawsuit may be filed within three years from the date when the plaintiff becomes aware of the infringement and the infringer, and in any case no later than five years from the date of the infringement. The procedure is urgent. The regulations on civil litigation procedure and on securing claims apply in the proceedings for protection of rights. The court may suspend the procedure due to infringement of the right of a filed industrial design until a decision for granting the right is adopted by the Office.

496. Within ninety days of the date of delivering the legally effective judgment accepting the lawsuit claims, the plaintiff may request to be registered in the relevant register as a holder of the right and to be issued the appropriate document by the Office. If the person does not submit a request for the granted right, the right shall be deleted from the relevant register.

497. The rights the third party has acquired from the former holder of the rights shall be valid for the new holder of the rights if they were registered in the relevant register or were duly reported for registration prior to the commencement of the dispute.

498. The court in some cases can order certain measures (Articles 313–315). In case when the person provides evidence that his right has been infringed or will be infringed, the court upon his proposal may determine temporary measures to secure his requests as follows:

- prohibit all infringing activities and their continuation;
- confiscate, remove from circulation and keep samples, means, equipment and related documents; and
- adopt other similar measures.

499. In addition, when the infringement is done while performing business activities for the purpose of gaining financial benefit and such infringement may cause irreparable harm, the court may set as a guarantee the confiscation of movable and immovable assets owned by the defendant and assets that are not directly related to the infringement, as well as a ban for disposing of finances on the accounts within financial institutions or disposing of other property.

500. If requested by the person whose right is infringed or there is justified doubt that his right will be infringed, the court may order a measure for providing evidence, especially regarding:

- preparation of a detailed description of the goods that have likely infringed the right with or without taking a sample;
- confiscation of the goods which is believed to have infringed the right;
- confiscation of materials and means used for preparation and distribution of goods believed to infringe the right, as well as related documentation.

501. When the party in the legal procedure relies on evidence and claims that that evidence is with the opposing party or under its control, the court shall invite the opposing party to provide such evidence specifying the time limit for submitting it. Where the party invited to provide evidence denies that they have the evidence or that it is under their control, the court may present evidence for determining the facts.

502. In addition to the civil protection, the right holder can request inspection relating to the circulation and use of protected industrial property rights, by the State Market Inspectorate (Articles 317–320). The Inspectorate can take a range of measures, including seizing infringing products, prohibiting the use of infringing means and equipment, and issuing to the infringing party a temporary suspension of business activities. The LIP contains provisions on misdemeanours and corresponding sanctions, primarily fines (Articles 321–322v).

§10. Overlapping and Relation to Other Intellectual Property Laws

503. Industrial design is one of the industrial property rights regulated with the LIP. As such, certain provisions regarding the procedural aspects, the registering agents, judicial protection, and others apply to all industrial property rights. Industrial design has similarities and certain overlaps with copyright, which is regulated by a different law (CL). The similarity is present primarily in the subject matter of protection, and in the scope of the rights. Under copyright law, a copyright work can be, among others, a work of applied art and design. Industrial design protects a design that is new and individual and applies to the outer appearance of industrial or handcrafted products. Therefore, at least in theory, it is possible that one product can enjoy a double protection under copyright and under industrial design. In addition, both copyright works and industrial designs are created by authors, who enjoy moral and exploitation rights. While the substance of the rights differs, the entitlement to moral rights in both cases implies that there is an individual link between the author and the copyright work or the industrial design.

Chapter 6. Plant Variety Protection

§1. Sources – Legislation

504. The plant variety in North Macedonia is protected by the Law on the Breeders' Rights, adopted in 2009.[165] This Law regulates the procedure and the conditions for grant, protection and termination of breeders' rights. The purpose of the Law is to grant breeders' rights and protect breeders' rights.

505. Specific plant genera and species to which the legal protection under the Law applies are designated in a list that is adopted by the Minister of Agriculture, Forestry and Water Economy.

506. In addition, there are a number of by-laws regulating the technicalities around filing the application, procedural elements, fees, etc. The by-laws are adopted by the Minister of Agriculture.

§2. Subject Matter of Protection

507. The Law defines in Article 4 who is considered as breeder:

(1) the person who bred, or discovered and developed, a variety;
(2) the person who is the employer of the aforementioned person or who has commissioned the latter's work; or
(3) the successor in title of these persons.

508. The Law also defines the term 'variety', which means a plant grouping within a single botanical taxon of the lowest known rank, the grouping of which, irrespective of whether the conditions for the grant of a breeder's right are fully met, can be defined by the expression of the characteristics resulting from a given genotype or combination of genotypes, distinguished from any other plant grouping by the expression of at least one of the said characteristics and considered as a unit with regard to its suitability for being propagated without changes.

509. It is specified that the provisions of the Law shall apply to at least fifteen plant genera and species designated by the Minister of Agriculture, Forestry and Water Economy based on genera and species that are of economic interest for the Republic of Macedonia, following a proposal by a commission of experts in this area.

510. The Law grants national treatment to nationals of a member of UPOV, contracting parties to international agreements to which the Republic of Macedonia is party to, as well as domestic and resident foreign natural persons and legal entities

---

165. Official Journal No. 52/2009.

having their registered offices within the territory of a member of UPOV, with respect to the grant and protection of breeders' rights.

§3. Conditions of Protection

511. The breeder's right shall be granted if the four cumulative conditions prescribed in Article 5 of the Law are met. These conditions require that the variety is:

(1) new. The variety shall be deemed to be new if, at the date of filing of the application for a breeder's right, propagating or harvested material of the variety has not been sold or otherwise disposed of to others, by or with the consent of the breeder, for purposes of exploitation of the variety, for no longer than one year in the territory of the Republic of Macedonia, or four years in a territory other than the Republic of Macedonia or six years in the case of trees or vines. In certain situations, defined in the Law, the variety will be considered new even when it has been disposed of;
(2) distinct. The variety shall be deemed to be distinct if it is clearly distinguishable from any other variety whose existence is a matter of common knowledge at the time of the filing of the application. Common knowledge would cover in particular the filing of an application for the granting of a breeder's right or for the entering of a variety in an official register of varieties, in any country, provided that the application leads to the granting of a right or to the entering of the variety in the official register;
(3) uniform. The variety shall be deemed to be uniform if, regardless of the variation that may be expected from the particular features of its propagation, it is sufficiently uniform in its essential features;
(4) stable. The variety shall be deemed to be stable if its essential features remain unchanged after repeated propagation or, in the case of a particular cycle of propagation, at the end of each such cycle.

512. The grant of the breeder's right shall not be subject to any further or different conditions, provided that the variety is designated by a denomination in accordance with the Law and the applicant complies with the formalities provided for in the Law and that he pays the required fees.

§4. Formalities (Procedure for Grant and Obtaining Protection)

513. The procedure is initiated by the breeder, who files an application for a breeder's right to the Seed and Seedlings Directorate (Articles 11–15). A fee needs to be paid when filing the application. Further details concerning the filing procedure are regulated in a by-law adopted by the Minister of Agriculture.

514. The breeder who has duly filed an application for the protection of a variety in one of the members of UPOV (the 'first application') shall, for the purpose of filing an application for the grant of a breeder's right for the same variety with the Seed and Seedlings Directorate (the 'subsequent application'), enjoy a right of priority for a maximum period of twelve months, counted from the date of filing of the first application. In order to benefit from the right of priority, the breeder shall, in the subsequent application, claim the priority of the first application. The breeder shall be allowed a period of two years after the expiration of the period of priority or, where the first application is rejected or withdrawn, a period of one year, in which to submit to the Seed and Seedlings Directorate any necessary information required for the purpose of examination.

515. The decision to grant a breeder's right shall require an examination for compliance with the conditions for protection. In the course of the examination, the Seed and Seedlings Directorate may grow the variety or carry out other necessary tests, instigate the growing of the variety or carry out other necessary tests, or take into account the results of growing tests or other trials which have already been carried out. For the purposes of examination, the Seed and Seedlings Directorate may require the breeder to furnish any necessary information, documents or material. The tests and trials are at the expense of the applicant, in the amount of the real costs.

516. On the basis of the completed examination of the application and the results submitted by the Directorate for Seed and Seedlings, the Minister for Agriculture, Forestry and Water Economy issues a decision for granting or rejecting breeding rights. The holder of the right is obliged to pay an annual fee for maintaining the right.

517. The state provides measures designed to safeguard the interests of the breeder in the period between the filing of the application for the grant of a breeder's right and the grant of that right. Such measures entitle the breeder to equitable remuneration from any person who, during the said period, has carried out acts which, once the right is granted, require the breeder's authorization.

§5. Ownership and Transfer (Assignment – Licences)

518. The Law does not contain any provisions regarding transfer of rights. Those matters are subject to the general rules applicable to contracts, other types of transfer of ownership, succession, etc.

§6. Scope of Exclusive Rights

519. The breeders' rights are defined in Article 16. They cover several groups of acts:

(1) Acts in respect of the propagating material of the protected variety that require the authorization of the breeder:
   - production or reproduction,

- conditioning for the purpose of propagation,
- offering for sale,
- selling or other marketing,
- exporting,
- importing,
- storage for any of the purposes mentioned above.

  The breeder may make his authorization subject to conditions and limitations.

(2) Acts in respect of the harvested material, covering all the acts listed above in point (1) with respect to harvested material, including entire plants and parts of plants, obtained through the unauthorized use of propagating material of the protected variety, shall require the authorization of the breeder, unless the breeder has given reasonable opportunity to exploit the right in relation to the said propagating material.

(3) Acts related to basic, derived and certain other varieties. The same provisions as in points (1) and (2) also apply in relation to:

- varieties which are essentially derived from the protected variety, where the protected variety is not itself an essentially derived variety;
- varieties which are not clearly distinguishable from the protected variety; and
- varieties whose production requires the repeated use of the protected variety.

  A variety shall be deemed to be essentially derived from another variety ('the initial variety') when it is predominantly derived from the initial variety, or from a variety that is itself predominantly derived from the initial variety while retaining the expression of the essential characteristics that result from the genotype or combination of genotypes of the initial variety; it is clearly distinguishable from the initial variety; and, except for the differences which result from the act of derivation, it conforms to the initial variety in the expression of the essential characteristics that result from the genotype or combination of genotypes of the initial variety.

520. Essentially derived varieties may be obtained, for example, by the selection of a natural or induced mutant, or of a somaclonal variant, the selection of a variant individual from plants of the initial variety, backcrossing, or transformation by genetic engineering.

§7. Limitations of the Scope of Protection – Compulsory Licences

521. Exceptions to the breeders' rights are stipulated in Article 17. The breeder's right shall not extend to:

(1) acts done privately and for non-commercial purposes;
(2) acts done for experimental purposes;

(3) acts done for the purpose of breeding other varieties, and, except where the provisions of Article 16(3) apply, acts referred to in Article 16(1) and (2) in respect of such other varieties.

522. In relation to varieties included in a list of agricultural plants, the breeder's right shall not be infringed by small farmers who, within reasonable limits and subject to the safeguarding of the legitimate interests of the breeder, use for propagating purposes, on their own property, the product of the harvest which they have obtained by planting, on their own property, the protected variety. The varieties of fruit trees, ornamentals, vegetables and forest plants are excluded from this exception.

523. Exhaustion of the right is regulated in Article 18. The breeder's right shall not extend to acts concerning any material of the protected variety, or of a variety covered by the provisions of paragraph (3) of Article 16, which has been sold or otherwise marketed by the breeder or with his consent in the territory of the Republic of Macedonia, or any material derived from the said material, unless such acts involve further propagation of the variety in question or involve an export of material of the variety, which enables the propagation of the variety, into a country which does not protect varieties of the plant genus or species to which the variety belongs, except where the exported material is for final consumption purposes. 'Material' means, for the purposes of this provision:

- propagating material of any kind;
- harvested material, including entire plants and parts of plants; and
- any product made directly from the harvested material.

524. According to Article 19, except where expressly provided in the Law, the free exercise of a breeder's right shall not be restricted in the territory of the Republic of Macedonia for reasons other than of public interest. When any such restriction has the effect of authorizing a third party to perform any act for which the breeder's authorization is required, the breeder shall receive equitable remuneration, according to law.

525. Article 20 specifies that the breeder's right shall be independent of any measure taken by the Republic of Macedonia to regulate within its territory the production, certification and marketing of material of varieties or the importing or exporting of such material. In any case, such measures shall not affect the application of the Law.

§8. Duration of Protection

526. The breeder's right, pursuant to Article 21, shall be valid for twenty years from the date of the grant of the breeder's right. For trees and vines, the validity period shall be twenty-five years from the said date.

527. In certain situations, defined in Article 23, the breeder's right shall be declared null and void. This is the case when it is established that:

i. the conditions laid down in Articles 6 and 7 were not complied with at the time of the grant of the breeder's right;
ii. where the grant of the breeder's right has been essentially based upon information and documents furnished by the breeder, the conditions laid down in Articles 8 or 9 were not complied with at the time of the grant of the breeder's right; or
iii. the breeder's right has been granted to a person who is not entitled to it, unless it is transferred to the person who is so entitled.

528. In addition, in certain situations the breeder's right can be cancelled. Under Article 24, this can happen if:

(a) it is established that the conditions laid down in Articles 8 or 9 are no longer fulfilled;
(b) after being requested to do so within the period of six months:
  – the breeder does not provide the Seed and Seedlings Directorate with the information, documents or material deemed necessary for verifying the maintenance of the variety;
  – the breeder fails to pay fees to keep his right in force; or
  – the breeder does not propose, where the denomination of the variety is cancelled after the grant of the right, another suitable denomination.

§9. Infringement and Remedies

529. The Law contains certain general provisions on remedies and judicial protection in Articles 26 and 27. The natural person or the legal entity that has violated the breeder's right is liable for compensation for damages according to the applicable legislation. The breeder whose rights have been violated may, in addition to the legal action for compensatory damages, also request an injunction to prohibit the committing of, or continuation of committing, the infringement of the breeder's right by suspension of the activity resulting in such infringement, and that the expenses of the proceedings for infringement be charged to the person or the legal entity who has violated the breeder's right. Breeder's right infringement shall refer to acts contrary to the breeder's rights as defined in Article 16.

530. The judicial protection for infringement of the breeder's right provided in Article 16 can be claimed within three years from the date the breeder has become aware of the infringement. After the expiration of the absolute term of five years after the infringement occurred, a lawsuit can no longer be submitted.

531. The State Agriculture Inspectorate, pursuant to Article 29, is responsible for administrative supervision over the application of Articles 16 and 17. If it suspects an infringement, it shall temporarily seize all items used, or intended for use, or resulting from the infringement.

§10. Overlapping and Relation to Other Intellectual Property Laws

532. While there are certain similarities between this right and industrial property rights, in terms of the elements of the procedure, priority right, scope of the rights, judicial protection, the plant variety protection is quite distinct. It is temporarily regulated in a separate law, and the institutions dealing with policymaking and with implementation and supervision in this area are completely different – Ministry of Agriculture, Seeds Directorate, and State Agriculture Inspectorate.

Chapter 7. Chip Protection

§1. Sources – Legislation

533. Chip protection is governed by the Law on protection of the topography of semiconductor products (Official Journal No. 05/98, 33/2006, 136/11, 53/2016). Other laws that regulate this area include the LIP. There are also by-laws, particularly a Rulebook specifying technical details about the application to register topographies at the Office. Regulations of general application, such as those on judicial protection, administrative procedure, or contracts, apply as well.

§2. Subject Matter of Protection

534. The subject matter of protection is the topography of semiconductor products. The Law in Article 2 provides definitions of semiconductor product and topography. Semiconductor product is defined as the final or intermediate form of any product intended to perform an electronic function and where there are elements, where at least one is active, and any or all of interconnectors are integrally established in a part of material or of the part of material, or in and on the part of material. The topography of semiconductor products is a three-dimensional layout of the elements expressed in any manner, where at least one is active, and of the interconnector in the semiconductor, or a three-dimensional layout prepared for production of a semiconductor product.

§3. Conditions of Protection

535. The Law provides for the conditions of protection in Article 8. A topography shall be protected if it is original. A topography is considered to be original if it is the result of its creator's own intellectual effort and was not commonplace in the semiconductor industry when it was created. Where a topography consists of elements that are commonplace in the respective industry, only the combination of those elements shall be protected, whereby it shall be presumed that it fulfils the originality criteria.

§4. Formalities (Procedure for Grant and Obtaining Protection)

536. The procedure for grant and obtaining protection is carried out by the Industrial Property Protection Office. The procedure is an administrative procedure, subject to the relevant rules, in particular the Law on General Administrative Procedure, and the Office concludes the procedure for granting and protection of topography by delivering a decision in the first instance (Article 6). This decision is subject to lodging an appeal within fifteen days from the day of receipt of the decision, to the State Commission deciding on administrative procedures and employment procedures in the second instance. The Office maintains the register of applications for granting topographies and the register of protected topographies (Article 7). These registers are public.

537. The procedure for protection and registration is provided in Articles 12–13a. The procedure for protection is initiated with an application that contains a request for granting the right and for entry into the register. The application shall contain information concerning the applicant and the creator, images of the topography with data about the sequences, an abstract relating to the characteristics of the electronic function or functions of the semiconductor, prepared on the basis of the protected topography, and if the topography has already been commercially exploited, a statement in writing relating to the date when it was first commercially exploited. A separate application is filed for each topography.

538. The Office examines whether the application contains all the elements needed for entry into the register of topographies. The request shall be rejected if the application does not contain all the prescribed elements. In case the application is partial, the Office shall invite the applicant to correct the application within two months. If the applicant fails to do so, the application shall be rejected. If the application contains all the elements, the Office shall take a decision to grant the right and enter it in the Register of Topographies. The entry in the respective register shall be published in the official journal of the Office.

539. The decision to grant the right is delivered by the Office within fifteen days from the day when the completed application was received. If the Office fails to deliver a decision within the deadline, the applicant is entitled within three days after the deadline to submit a request addressed to the Director to take the decision. The Director is obliged, within five working days from the date of submitting the request, to take a decision, either positive or negative. If the Director fails to take a decision, the applicant can notify the State Administrative Inspectorate within five working days, and the Inspectorate then makes an inspection and is authorized to take measures to order the Director to deliver a decision. As the last recourse in case of failure to act either by the Director or by the Inspectorate, the applicant can submit an application to the public prosecutor, or initiate an administrative court proceeding in case of absence of a decision in the matter. In case when the request to deliver a decision is rejected, the applicant is entitled to appeal within fifteen days, to the State Commission deciding on administrative procedure and employment procedure in the second instance.

540. A separate provision in Article 14 regulates the nullity of the registration. The registration is invalidated if it is established that: the respective topography is not original; or the application has not been filed by a natural or legal person who is entitled to the right to protection; or the application has been filed after the dates set out in the Law (Article 10(5) or Article 11); or the images of the protected topography do not allow its identification.

541. According to Article 11, the application for granting the right cannot be filed after the lapse of two years from the date when a topography was first commercially exploited.

§5. Ownership and Transfer (Assignment – Licences)

542. The right to protection of a topography is enjoyed by its creator (Article 3). When a topography is a product of several creators, the right of protection is enjoyed by all those persons. Where the topography is created in the course of the creator's employment or on the basis of an order, the right to protection shall be enjoyed by the creator's employer or person placing the order, unless the terms of employment or of the order provide otherwise. Under Article 4, foreign persons, with respect to the protection of topography, are entitled to the same rights as domestic persons, if it is according to international treaties and conventions or if it arises from the application of the principle of reciprocity. The person that relies on the principle of reciprocity has to prove the existence of reciprocity.

543. The Law does not contain provisions on transfer of the rights. There is only a reference in Article 18 to the LIP, stating that the rules on transfer and licences specified in that Law apply to topographies as well.

§6. Scope of Exclusive Rights

544. Pursuant to Article 9, the holder of the protected topography has the exclusive right of commercial exploitation, including the right to authorize or prohibit any of the following acts:

- reproduction of the topography by any means or in any form;
- importation, sale or other forms of distribution of the topography or semiconductor product incorporating the respective topography or products that include semiconductors and which incorporate the protected topography.

545. 'Commercial exploitation' of topography means the manufacture, sale, rental, leasing or any other method of commercial distribution directly related to the topography or to semiconductor products produced on the basis of the respective topography.

§7. Limitations of the Scope of Protection

546. Under Article 9, the exclusive right shall not extend to any concept, process, system or technic embodied in the topography other than the protected topography itself. The right is exhausted once the protected topography or semiconductor products are placed for use on the market by the right holder himself or with his authorization.

547. Article 15 specifies cases that shall not be considered an infringement of the right of protection of a protected topography:

– reproduction of a protected topography for non-commercial purposes; or
– reproduction of a protected topography with a purpose to analyse or evaluate its concept, processes, systems and technics, embodied in the topography, or for research or educational purposes; or
– commercial exploitation of a new topography which has been created on the basis of analyses and evaluation of protected topography, but is considered to be original and the result of its creator's own intellectual effort and is not commonplace in the semiconductor industry.

§8. Duration of Protection

548. Article 10 governs the validity of the right. A topography shall be protected when it is entered in the register of topographies. The holder of protected topography shall acquire his exclusive right on the date of filling the application, or on the date when the respective topography was first commercially exploited anywhere in the world. The exclusive right shall be valid for ten years starting from the earlier of the following dates:

– the end of the calendar year in which the topography is first commercially exploited anywhere in the world; or
– the end of the calendar year in which the application has been filed.

549. The exclusive right shall expire before this period if the administrative fees are not paid or if the right holder of the protected topography renounces the protection in writing. If a topography has not been commercially exploited, the exclusive right shall expire after fifteen years from its fixation or decoding. During the term of protection, the right holder is entitled to mark the respective semiconductor product with a capital 'T'.

§9. Infringement and Remedies

550. A person whose rights have been infringed may, in addition to damages, request that the person infringing his right be prohibited from carrying on the infringing acts (Article 15). Any person who infringes the right of protection of a protected topography shall be liable for damage caused, in accordance with the general rules governing compensation for damages.

551. A person who commercially exploits a semiconductor product incorporating the protected topography, and did not know, or had no reasonable grounds to believe that the topography of the product is protected shall not be liable for compensation of damages (Article 16). The right holder of the protected topography is entitled to claim compensation for damages from the date when the person who commercially exploited the topography acquired knowledge that the topography is protected. The amount of compensation shall be agreed between the right holder and the person who exploited it. If no agreement is reached, the court shall establish the amount of compensation. These provisions apply also to the successors of the person exploiting the topography. The right of commercial exploitation is limited to importation, sale or distribution of the semiconductor products or other products incorporating the protected topography, and this right applies to a topography or products at the time when the claim for compensation was received.

§10. Overlapping and Relation to Other Intellectual Property Laws

552. Even though topographies are governed by a separate law, there are certain common rules with the industrial property rights governed by the LIP. The provisions from the LIP relating to representation, availability of documents and information by the Office, receipt of application, entry of data and changes in the register, rules on judicial protection, transfer of rights and licences, supervision, apply to topographies accordingly. Topographies, like the industrial property rights, are registered and maintained by the Office.

Chapter 8. Geographical Indications and Appellations of Origin

§1. Sources – Legislation

553. Main sources on geographical indications and appellations of origin in the Macedonian legislation include the LIP,[166] the LQAP,[167] Law on Wine,[168] as well as the Law on Agriculture and Rural Development (LARD).[169]

554. Concerning international conventions and agreements relevant to geographical indications and appellations of origin, Macedonia has acceded to the Lisbon Agreement for the Protection of Appellations of Origin and their International Registration and its Stockholm Act on 6 July 2010.[170] The country is party to the agreement on Trade-Related Aspects of Intellectual Property Rights (TRIPS Agreement) (1994)[171] as well as to the Central European Free Trade Agreement (CEFTA) from 2006.[172]

555. The LIP has been using the term 'geographical names' (Macedonian: *geografski nazivi)* that enhances the: (1) appellations of origin (Macedonian: *oznaki na poteklo*) and (2) the geographical indications (Macedonian: *geografski oznaki*).

556. Since 1993, the LIP stipulated the appellation of origin, which is considered as a higher type of protection. Starting from 2002, LIP apart from the appellation of origin, a new, a so-called 'lower protection', has also been introduced through a new institute – geographical indication, adopted under the influence of the legal terminology of the European Union.[173]

557. In October 2010, a special *LQAP* was adopted,[174] in order to foster national and international registration of protected geographical indications and protected

166. Official Journal Nos 21/09, 24/11, 12/14, 41/14, 152/15, 53/16, 83/18, 31/20.
167. Official Journal Nos 140/10, 53/11, 55/12, 106/13, 116/15, 149/15,.193/15, 39/16.
168. Official Journal Nos 50/10, 53/11, 6/12, 23/13, 106/13, 188/13, 149/15, 39/16, 172/16.
169. Official Journal Nos 49/10, 53/11, 126/12, 15/13, 69/13, 106/13, 177/14, 25/15, 73/15, 83/15, 154/15, 11/16, 53/16, 120/16, 163/16.
170. Official Journal No. 77/2010.
171. Official Journal of the Republic of Macedonia, No. 07/03.
172. Official Journal No. 59/2006.
173. For detailed elaboration of the Macedonian legislation on geographical indications *see* Y. Reboul, Polenak Akimovska, G. Naumovski: *Introduction to Trademarks and Geographical Indications*, Tempus project 144582, Faculty of Law Iustinianus Primus, Skopje, 2010; G. Naumovski, *Geographical Indications in Macedonian Law*, WIPO Research Papers from the WIPO-WTO Colloquium for Teachers of Intellectual Property Law, Geneva, 2010, p. 69–80.
174. Official Journal No. 140/10.

designations of origin for agricultural products. This law also introduced the traditional speciality guaranteed (Macedonian: Oznaka za garantiran tradicionalen specijalitet) for traditional agricultural and food products with acknowledged special features.[175] LQAP was amended[176] for the purpose of alignment with the EU Regulation 1151/2012.

558. An important basis concerning GIs of wines is the *Law on Wine (LW)* which includes additional regulations contained in Chapter V ('classification of wine, production, designation and protection of wine with geographical indication'). LW has a '*lex specialis*' character; i.e., it overrides LIP and LQAP, regarding the geographical indications for wines.

559. From the aspect of economic importance and the functions of the geographical indications and appellations of origin, the provisions of the LARD[177] are also relevant. In this sense, LARD stipulates that the agricultural products of higher quality are those made by applications of standards for: guaranteed traditional uniqueness, geographical indications and appellation of origin protection and wine with geographical origin.[178] LARD also provides mechanisms for state financial aid for introduction of higher quality standards for making these products.[179]

560. As far as the secondary legislation is concerned, the following by-laws of particular relevance have been adopted: Regulation on Appellations of Origin and Geographical Indications, enacted by the SOIP.[180] Furthermore, the regulations concerning geographical indications and appellations of origin under the LQAP, enacted by the Ministry of Agriculture, Forestry and Water of the Republic of Macedonia are relevant, namely: Regulation on the form and content of the application for registration of a designation of origin or geographical indication;[181] Regulation on the form and content of the elaborate contained in the application for registration of a designation of origin or geographical indication;[182] Regulation on the form and content of the single document from the application for registration of a designation of origin or geographical indication;[183] Regulation on the costs in the procedure for registration and use of the designation of origin, the geographical indication and the designation for guaranteed traditional speciality;[184] Regulation on the form, content, size and use of the marks and marks 'protected designation of origin', 'protected geographical indication' and 'designation of a guaranteed traditional

175. LQAP, Arts 2, 71.
176. Official Journal Nos 53/11, 55/12, 106/13, 116/15, 149/15, 193/15, 39/16.
177. Official Journal Nos 49/10, 53/11, 126/12, 15/13, 69/13, 106/13, 177/14, 25/15, 73/15, 83/15, 154/15, 11/16, 53/16, 120/16, 163/16.
178. LARD, Arts 74, 10.
179. LARD, Art. 106.
180. Official Journal No. 102/2009.
181. Official Journal No. 77/2012.
182. Official Journal Nos 100/2012.
183. Official Journal No. 99/2011.
184. Official Journal No. 123/2012.

specialty';[185] Decision for determination of the agricultural and food products that are protected on national and international level by protection of the geographical name with designation of origin or geographical indication and protection of the traditional name with designation of guaranteed traditional specialty;[186] Regulation on the form of the objection to the proposed name from the request for registration of a designation of origin, geographical indication or designation for a guaranteed traditional specialty and the form for submission of information from the settlement procedure; Regulation on the form, content, and manner of submitting the request for annulment of the registration decision;[187] Regulation on the manner of submitting the request and the form and content of the application form for amendment and supplementation of the report or specification;[188] and Regulation on the form and content of the register of authorized verification bodies.[189] When it comes to wines, secondary legislation includes: the Rules on indication of the geographical areas suitable for production of wine with geographical name[190] and the Rules on classification of recommended and approved grape varieties for production of every vineyard area for production of wine,[191] as well documents concerning the procedure, such as the Rules for Content and form for the Elaboration of Production and Labeling of Wine with Geographical Name, the Rules on the content and form of the Register of Wine with Protected Geographical Names and of Users of the Geographical Names, the Form of the Application, the Procedure for Inscription and the Required Documentation.[192]

§2. Subject Matter of Protection

561. LIP stipulates that the geographical name – in Macedonian: *geografski naziv* – shall be protected by an appellation of origin of the product and a geographical indication.[193] The geographical name is indicated on the products produced by natural or legal persons in a certain geographical area.[194]

562. LIP defines the appellation of origin – in Macedonian: *oznaka na potekloto* – as the geographical name of the country, region or place indicated on the product originating from that area and having quality and particular characteristics exclusively or mostly conditioned by the geographical environment, including the natural and human factors and the production, processing and preparation which are entirely carried out in the certain limited region of origin.[195] Except for wine and

185. Official Journal No. 24/2012.
186. Official Journal No. 89/2012.
187. Official Journal No. 128/2012.
188. Official Journal No. 100/2012.
189. Official Journal No. 101/2011.
190. Official Journal 48/11, 113/11.
191. Official Journal 89/12.
192. Official Journal, No. 71/11, 61/14.
193. LIP, Art. 226(1).
194. LIP, Art. 226(2).
195. LIP, Art. 227.

other alcoholic drinks, the product may be indicated with an appellation of origin even if raw materials for its production originate from a wider area or out of the area of processing provided that:(1) the defined area for raw materials production is limited or if there are special conditions for raw materials production and (2) the traditional method of production, i.e., the human factor, is crucial for the quality and special characteristics of the product.[196]

563. On the other hand, the geographical indication – in Macedonian: *geografska oznaka* – is the geographical name of the country, the region, or place indicated on the product having quality, reputation or other characteristics that may be essentially attributed to the geographical origin. The geographical indication of a product may be protected provided that production and/or procedure and/or preparation of the product are carried out in a certain place of origin. The geographical names that do not meet the requirements for protection as an appellation of origin may be protected as geographical indications.[197]

564. LIP also contains a provision on traditional names, prescribing that a geographical name will also be considered the name that does not include a geographical name of a certain country, region or place, which after long market sale has become generally known as a traditional name for the product originating from that territory, as well as the historical name of that territory referring to a definite origin of the product, that fulfils the requirements for geographical indication and appellation of origin.[198]

565. Concerning the scope of protection, according to LIP, a geographical name may be used for marking natural products, agricultural products, industrial products, handicraft products and homemade handworks.[199]

566. According to LQAP, the protection and the registration of the geographical or traditional name of the agricultural and food products are possible with a designation of origin – Macedonian: oznaka na poteklo – a geographical indication – Macedonian: geografska oznaka – while traditional names are protected by guaranteed traditional speciality – Macedonian: garantiran tradicionalen specijalitet.[200]

567. Regarding geographical indications for wines, the LW defines the geographical indications (GIs) as 'name and/or the designation of the country, region or place designating that the product originates from that area'.[201] Furthermore, LW in terms of quality classifies the wine into four categories: (1) table wine; (2) regional wine (or table WGI); (3) wine with controlled origin (WCO), and (4) wine with controlled and guaranteed origin (WCGO).[202] Hence, according to LW, WGI,

196. LIP, Art. 229.
197. LIP, Art. 228.
198. LIP, Art. 230.
199. LIP, Art. 231.
200. LQAP, Art. 1.
201. LW, Art. 3(27).
202. LW, Art. 38(1).

WCI and WCGO are considered 'wines with geographical name'.[203] LW classifies the areas suitable for 'wines with geographical names' into regions, vineyards and localities, habitats, and limited vines-growing units.[204]

§3. Conditions of Protection

I. Geographical Names under LIP

568. A geographical indication, i.e., appellation of origin, may not protect the product name which: (1) does not fulfil the requirements under LIP; (2) is contrary to the law and morality; (3) by its content may be misleading as to the kind, origin, quality, manner of production or other properties of the product; (4) is equal to the name of a plant variety or animal breed, in case when it might mislead the public regarding the geographical origin; (5) although presents the exact name of the country, region or place of product it may provoke false impression to the customer that the product originates from other country, region or place; (6) is not protected in the country of origin or ceased to be used in the country of origin, and (7) is identical or similar to the geographical name or trademark registered previously for identical or similar products, when there is probability to mislead the customer.[205]

569. Furthermore, geographical indication, i.e., appellation of origin, may not protect the name of place of origin originally used for indicating products of that place of origin, but after long market sale has become generic, i.e., generally known for indicating a definite kind of products.[206]

570. The name of the place of origin protected by geographical indication, or an appellation of origin, may not become generic.[207]

571. Concerning the homonyms, LIP prescribes that if the names of two or more places of origin of products are identical or almost identical, in writing, the protection of such names with geographical indication or appellation of origin shall be approved to all persons that meet the requirements under LIP, and if these names are used in accordance with good business practices as well as on the principle of equality of the producers at the market and truthful informing of the customer, except if it might mislead the public regarding the geographical origin.[208]

572. Regarding international protection, the geographical name which is already protected by geographical indication, i.e., appellation of origin in the Republic of

203. LW, Art. 39(1).
204. LW, Art. 39(2).
205. LIP, Art. 232.
206. LIP, Art. 233(1).
207. LIP, Art. 233(2).
208. LIP, Art. 234.

Macedonia, may be protected abroad on the ground of bilateral agreement for mutual protection or international agreements ratified by the Republic of Macedonia.[209]

573. The application for protection out of the country may be submitted merely by users of geographical names registered in the register of protected geographical names of SOIP.[210]

574. Geographical name may also be protected by a foreign natural or legal person or a group of producers by registering an authorized user of the protected geographical name in case when it results from international agreements ratified by the Republic of Macedonia or based on bilateral agreements for mutual protection if it is provided in the legislation of the country of origin of that person.[211]

II. Geographical Names under LQAP

575. As far as the definitions of geographical names for agricultural products and foodstuffs are concerned, 'geographical name' is the name and/or landmark of the place, region or country with which they indicate that the product originates in that area. LAQP defines 'Geographical indication' as the name of a region, a specific place or, in exceptional cases, a country which used to denote agricultural or food products whose production and/or processing and/or preparation take place in that geographical area.[212] Hence, the designation of origin may protect the name of the agricultural and foodstuffs: (1) originating from a specific place, region or in exceptional cases a country; (2) whose quality or characteristics, for the most part or exclusively, are influenced by special natural human factors in a particular geographical area; and (3) all production processes take place entirely in a defined geographical area.[213]

576. On the other hand, the name of the agricultural and food product can be protected with a geographical indication for products: (1) originating from a specific place, region, or country; (2) which have a specific quality, reputation or other feature that is attributed to the geographical origin and (3) at least one of the production processes takes place in a defined geographical area.[214]

577. Concerning the relations with trademarks, LQAP promulgates that when the application for trademark registration is submitted after the day of submission, the application for designation of origin and the geographical indications are registered in accordance with the provisions of LQAP and the regulations adopted on the basis thereof, the request for trademark registration will be denied. However, the

209. LIP, Art. 235(1).
210. LIP, Art. 235(2).
211. LIP, Art. 235(3).
212. LQAP, Art. 2 (67–68).
213. LQAP, Art. 142(1).
214. LQAP, Art. 142(2).

trademark registered on the territory of the Republic of Macedonia in accordance with special regulations, before the date of submission of the application for registration of designation of origin or geographical indication, may continue to be used.[215]

III. Geographical Names under LW

578. The Rules on indication of the geographical areas suitable for production of wine with geographical name[216] prescribe designating the geographical area for production of wines with geographical name, according to a List of Geographical Areas in the following way: (1) region, as a geographical area of origin of regional wine or table WGI, which is the entire territory of the Republic of Macedonia; (2) vineyards, being geographical area for WCO; and (3) localities, habitats, and limited vines-growing units as geographical areas suitable for production of WCGO.[217]

579. In this sense, according to the Rules, wines produced from vines-growing areas on the territory of the Republic of Macedonia can carry the protected name 'Macedonia' and be designated as 'Regional Wine Macedonia' and/or 'MACEDONIAN REGIONAL WINE' (in Macedonian: *Заштитено име: Македонија, Употреба: Регионално вино Македонија и/или Македонско регионално вино, Територија: Република Македонија*). Furthermore, WCO can be produced in one of the sixteen vineyard (geographical) areas (Skopje, Veles, Tikvesh, Gevgelija-Valandovo, Strumica-Radovish, Ovhe pole, Kochani-Vinica, Kumanovo, Kratovo, Pijanec, Prilep, Bitola, Prespa, Ohrid, Kichevo, and Tetovo).[218] As far as WCGO are concerned, they originate from numerous localities, habitats, and limited vines-growing units.[219]

580. Although Macedonian GI legislation follows international and European standards, IP academia and practitioners in Macedonia on several occasions have outlined that the provisions of the LW and different by-laws enacted under its authority do not offer particularly clear legal standing when the regulation of GIs for wine is concerned and that there is a need for further clarification and elaboration of applicable rules.[220]

---

215. LQAP, Art. 157.
216. Official Journal 48/11, 113/11.
217. *See* List of Geographical Areas suitable for production of wines with geographical name, Annex to the Rules on indication of the geographical areas suitable for production of wine with geographical name (Official Journal 48/11, 113/11.).
218. *Ibid.*
219. For analysis of the importance of the GI protection for the wine industry in Macedonia, as well as the characteristics of the regime for protection of GIs in the LW, *see* Buchkovski, V., Gavrilovikj N., Naumovski G., Vuchen F.: Geographical Indications Protection in the Republic of Macedonia with reference to wines, *Intellectual Property, Innovation And Science In A Global Environment,* Collection with Papers of the Fifth National Seminar with International Participation, University of Library Studies and Information Technologies, University Youth Knowledge Academy, Sofia, 2017.
220. *Ibid.*

§4. FORMALITIES (PROCEDURE FOR GRANT AND OBTAINING PROTECTION)

I. Procedures According to LIP

A. Registration of Geographical Names

581. As far as the initiation of procedure is concerned, the procedure for geographical name protection is initiated by application which contains a request for geographical name protection, i.e., request for granting the right to use the protected geographical name and other supplements provided by law.[221]

582. A foreign person can also submit the application. In this case, with the request for protection of a geographical name, the applicant has to enclose a copy of a certificate or other legal act in the official language of the country of origin, issued by the competent authority in the country of origin, as an evidence that the geographical name is protected in that country, in accordance with the national legislation in the country of origin as well as a certified translation in the Macedonian language.[222]

583. One application may refer to protection of only one geographical name relating to only one type of product.[223]

584. Application for protection of geographical name may be filed by: (1) natural or legal persons producing, on a certain geographical area, a product indicated by the name of that area, and a group of producers and manufacturers of the same products irrespective of the composition and form of joining; (2) state administrative body, local self-government unit and chambers interested in protection of geographical names in the area of their activity; (3) foreign natural and legal persons, i.e., foreign groups of producers, only if the right of authorized user for the protected geographical name has been granted in the countries of origin and if they fulfil the requirements under this LIP.[224]

585. An application for protection of geographical name shall contain a request for protection of the geographical name with a designation whether protection with the appellation of origin or with a geographical indication is requested. An application for protection of geographical name with an appellation of origin or with a geographical indication, besides the request for protection of geographical name, shall contain a study of the product, i.e., to be indicated with the geographical name. The contents and form of the application referred to, the study and the other components and supplements shall be prescribed in a regulation adopted by the director of SOIP.[225]

---

221. LIP, Art. 236.
222. LIP, Art. 237.
223. LIP, Art. 238.
224. LIP, Art. 239.
225. LIP, Art. 240.

586. For the purpose of the procedure, a study must be prepared by an institution which fulfils the requirements provided by the Regulation on Appellations of Origin and Geographical Indications.[226] The control of the special characteristics of the product may be carried out by the institution which has elaborated the study, or on the request of one party, by other institution which fulfils the requirements provided for in a regulation adopted by the director of SOIP, for which evidence is issued. The institution which has elaborated the study within ninety days of protecting the geographical name should constitute a commission for controlling the quality and the special characteristics of the product which will be indicated with the geographical name. The Commission referred shall consist of five members who have participated in elaborating the study and/or other persons having knowledge in the field of the product concerned. At least one member of the Commission should be a manufacturer.[227]

587. If the institution which has elaborated the study within the prescribed period cannot constitute a commission for controlling the quality and the special characteristics of the product, it shall propose another relevant institution, no later than ninety days of the date of protecting the geographical name. If the institution which has elaborated the study within the prescribed time limit fails to act, SOIP shall request an opinion from professional institutions depending on the kind of product or from group of producers of the relevant product, for a proposal of a new institution for product control.[228]

588. Amending the study is also possible, i.e., natural or legal persons and associations of legal and natural persons that fulfil the requirements for an applicant according to LIP and have legal interest may request amending the study as a result of changes arising from the development of science and technical knowledge or because of redefining the borders of the geographical area. The request for amending the study shall be submitted to the institution which has elaborated it or to another institution which fulfils the requirements prescribed in a regulation adopted by the director of SOIP. The request for amending the study should contain the reasons for the requested changes. The applicant should submit the amendment to the study to SOIP. As a change of the study shall also be considered the change of the institution for product control.[229]

589. SOIP shall keep a register of applications for protection of geographical names and a register of applications for using the protected geographical names, a register of protected geographical names and a register of users of protected geographical names. The contents and the method of keeping the registers are prescribed by the Regulation on Appellations of Origin and Geographical

226. Official Journal, 102/2009.
227. LIP, Art. 241.
228. LIP, Art. 242.
229. LIP, Art. 243.

Indications.[230] On a written request of the persons concerned, SOIP shall issue copies of documents, certificates, and extracts from the registers.[231]

590. The acquisition of right to the name of the place of origin for products with geographical indication, i.e., appellation of the origin, is made by positive decision and registering the geographical name of the product and the kind of the product the name in the register of protected geographical names refers to.[232] The publishing of a protected geographical name in the official newsletter of SOIP is ex officio, as prescribed by the Regulation on Appellations of Origin and Geographical Indications.[233]

B. Granting the Right of Authorized User

591. Since the appellations of origin and the geographical indications are collective rights, their use is granted in a procedure which if it is successful results in granting of the right of authorized user of registered geographical names, i.e., authorized users of appellation of origin and users of geographical indications.

592. The appellation of origin shall be a collective right and may be used exclusively by legal and natural persons and associations of legal and natural persons who: (1) produce or process a product the geographical name of which is protected by an appellation of origin; (2) carry out the whole process of production in a geographical area which is precisely defined in the study; and (3) are registered in the register of users as users of that appellation of origin.[234]

593. The geographical indication shall be a collective right and may be used by legal and natural persons who: (1) produce a product with a geographical name protected by a geographical indication; (2) perform production and/or processing and/or preparation of the product in a geographical area which is precisely defined in the study; and (3) are registered in the register of users as users of that geographical indication.[235]

594. The application for granting of the right of usage contains: (1) a request for granting the right to use protected geographical name; (2) evidence for performing specific activity; and (3) evidence for performed control. The contents and form of application are prescribed in the Regulation on Appellations of Origin and Geographical Indications.[236]

---

230. Official Journal, 102/2009.
231. LIP, Art. 244.
232. LIP, Art. 245.
233. LIP, Art. 254.
234. LIP, Art. 247.
235. *Ibid.*
236. LIP, Art. 248.

595. If SOIP determines that the application does not meet the requirements for protection of the geographical name, it shall, in writing, inform the applicant of the reasons for not protecting the geographical will and call the applicant within ninety days from the date of receiving the notification to explain the reasons (upon elaborated request from the applicant, for justified reasons, the time limit may be renewed for another ninety days at the latest).[237] If the applicant within the prescribed time limit provides no explanation at all or provides an explanation, and SOIP determines that the geographical name cannot be protected it shall, by a decision, reject the application for protection of geographical name, i.e., the application for granting the right of authorized user of the geographical name.[238]

596. If the application is in accordance with LIP and the regulations, SOIP further examines in order to check if it fulfils the requirements for granting the right of authorized user.[239] If the application for granting the right of authorized user of the geographical name fulfils the requirements provided for in this Law, SOIP shall advise the applicant, within thirty days, to pay the fee for granting the right of authorized user of geographical name for the first five years, the costs for publishing of the information for the granted right to use the protected geographical name, as well as for issuing certificate, and to submit an evidence for the services performed.[240] If the applicant submits evidence for the payments, SOIP shall make a decision for granting the right of authorized user and shall register it in the register of users of protected geographical names and in the register for protected geographical names.[241]

597. After the payment for the costs of publishing by the holder of the right for authorized user, SOIP shall publish the information for granting the right of authorized user in the newsletter.[242] SOIP issues the authorized user of protected geographical name a certificate for granted right of authorized user within six months from the date of taking the decision.[243]

II. Procedures for Geographical Names for Agricultural Products

598. The procedure for protection of geographical indications and appellations of origin for agricultural products is under the competence of the Ministry of Agriculture, Forestry and Water Economy, in accordance with the provisions of LQAP

237. LIP, Art. 251.
238. Additionally, if there is an application for protection of geographical name with appellation of origin and SOIP finds that the criteria for appellation of origin are not fulfilled, but the requirements to be protected by geographical indication are satisfied, the Office shall inform the applicant and, with his consent, shall protect the geographical name by a geographical indication.
239. LIP. Art. 250.
240. LIP, Art. 252(2).
241. LIP, Art. 253.
242. LIP, Art. 255.
243. LIP, Art. 256.

and the *Regulation on the form and content of the elaborate contained in the application for registration of a designation of origin or geographical indication.*[244]

599. The elaborate contains the following elements: (1) name of the agricultural or food product which contains a designation of origin or geographical indication; (2) description of the agricultural or food product, raw material, as well as the main physical, chemical, microbiological or organoleptic characteristics of agricultural or food product; (3) defining the geographical area; (4) proof that the agricultural or food product originates from the determined geographical area; (5) description of the production method including the way of packaging if the same is obligatorily performed in the defined geographical area for the needs of protection of the quality and origin of the product and its control of agricultural or food product and, if necessary, the authentic and immutable local production method; (6) data on: connection between the quality or the characteristics of the agricultural or food product and geographical area or connection between the specific quality, reputation or other characteristics of the agricultural or the foodstuff with the geographical area referred; (7) name and address of the authorized bodies that verify the conformity of the product with the report and (8) specific rules for labelling of agricultural or food product.[245]

600. An application for registration can be submitted by an interested group of operators who are engaged in the production, processing or trade of the same agricultural or foodstuff product regardless of their legal form or composition. Other interested subjects can also participate in the group of manufacturers.[246] LQAP in detail regulates the procedure for review of the application by a special committee,[247] the opposition procedure including settlement procedures,[248] the decision for protection and registration, the geographical names' registers and the initial and additional/subsequent right of use,[249] amendment and supplements to the elaboration,[250] annulation of registration decisions,[251] the use of the indications (protected designation of origin – PDO; protected geographical indication – PDI, and traditional speciality guaranteed – TSG; Macedonian: Zaštitena oznaka na poteklo; Zaštitena geografska oznaka; Oznaka za garantiran tradicionalen specijalitet),[252] the costs for the procedure.[253]

601. The detailed issues are regulated by the secondary legislation (Rules) enacted by the Ministry of Agriculture, Forestry and Water Economy, mentioned in § 1 (Sources – Legislation).

---

244. Official Journal No. 100/2012.
245. LQAP, Art. 145.
246. LQAP, Art. 147.
247. LQAP, Art. 148.
248. LQAP, Art. 149.
249. LQAP, Arts 150, 151.
250. LQAP, Art. 152.
251. LQAP, Art. 153.
252. LQAP, Art. 154.
253. LQAP, Art. 155.

602. The relevant compliance controls are realized by certification bodies, accredited by the Institute of Accreditation of Macedonia.[254]

603. LQAP also regulates the international registration of geographical names on the bases of bilateral mutual agreements for protection or international agreements ratified by the Republic of Macedonia, as well as on the basis of a submitted request for protection in accordance with the regulations of the country in which it is performed protection[255] as well as the registration on an EU level.[256]

III. Procedures for Geographical Names for Wine

A. Registration of Wine with Protected Geographical Names

604. The procedure is initiated upon an application for inscription in the Register of Wine with Protected Geographical Names. The application must contain an elaboration in which the following issues are determined: (1) geographical area of production; (2) sorting and methods of vine cultivation; (3) maximum yield per hectare; (4) areas and methods of vinification; (5) appropriate parameters of physical-chemical and organoleptic characteristics.[257]

605. Within thirty days of the receipt of the application for inscription, the Ministry enacts a decision for approval of the request inscription in the register, or a decision for rejection of the request.[258]

606. For the other procedural issues regarding the registration, the provisions of LQAP are applied regarding the availability of the geographical names, the procedure for examination of the application, the opposition procedure, the decision of approval or rejection of the application, the acquisition and the subsequent right to use, the amendment and supplement of the Elaboration, the revoking of the registration, the negative entitlements, and the symbols for PDOs and PDGs.[259]

B. Right to Use the Registered Wine Geographical Name

607. When the request for inscription of a geographical name in the register has been approved, the wine producers that have submitted the request (applicants with approved request) are entitled to use the registered geographical name;[260] i.e., they are authorized users of the geographical name. Additionally, any other wine producer that by elaboration subsequently proves that the wine is produced according

254. LQAP, 161, 162.
255. LQAP, Art. 158.
256. LQAP, Art. 159.
257. LW, Art. 42.
258. LW, Art. 42-a (1–2).
259. LWAP, Arts 141, 142, 144, 147–154, 156.
260. LW, Art. 42-a (4).

to the conditions for production of wine with protected geographical name can become a user of the registered geographical name.[261] The procedure is regulated by the Rules on the content and form of the Register of Wine with Protected Geographical Names and of Users of the Geographical Names, the Form of the Application, the Procedure for Inscription, and the Required Documentation.[262]

608. LW provisions also include a reference that the wine and other wine grape products on the market must be labelled to provide protection of consumers' interest and competition protection,[263] as well as clear provisions on the definition and elements of the label, especially when it comes to labels for wines with geographical names.[264]

609. LW furthermore notes that in accordance with Articles 23, 24 and 25 of the Trade-Related Aspects of Intellectual Property Rights, as well as Article 4 of Annex 2 of Additional Protocol for Wine and the Stabilization and Association Agreement,[265,266] the use in the Republic of Macedonia of geographical name wine that does not originate from the place indicated by the geographical indication or appellation of origin in question is prohibited, even where the true origin of the goods is indicated, but the geographical name is used in translation or accompanied by expressions such as 'kind', 'type', 'style', 'imitation' or 'similar'.[267]

§5. Ownership and Transfer (Assignment – Licences)

610. The right to use protected geographical name may not be assigned, derogated, or given in pawn by an agreement. If the protected geographical name is a subject of previously applied or registered trademark, such trademark may not be assigned, derogated, or given in pawn.[268]

§6. Scope of Exclusive Rights

611. The user of protected geographical name shall have the right to use it for indicating exclusively that kind of product which has been registered into the register of protected geographical names of SOIP. The right of use shall also refer to the usage of the protected geographical name on the packing, advertising materials, business identification documents and other business documentation, as well as import and export of products indicated by a geographical name. Authorized users

261. LW, Art. 42-1(5).
262. Official Journal, No. 71/11, 61/14.
263. LW, Art. 49(1).
264. LW, Arts 52–54.
265. Official Journal L 084, 20/03/2004 P. 0013–0197.
266. Official Journal of the European Communities L342/13.
267. LW, Art. 55.
268. LIP, Art. 258.

of protected geographical name shall have the exclusive right to indicate their products by 'Appellation of origin controlled' if authorized for using an appellation of origin or 'Geographical indication controlled' if authorized for using geographical indication.[269]

612. The users of the geographical names may request prohibition of: (1) direct or indirect unauthorized use of protected geographical name for equal or similar products for acquiring proprietary benefit; (2) marking the products not originating from the place of origin indicated by the protected geographical name even when real origin is indicated, its translation used or when used associated with additional expressions, like 'style', 'type', 'by method', 'as produced in', 'imitation', etc.; (3) any kind of use of the protected geographical name which harms the reputation or misuses the reputation of the protected geographical name; (4) any kind of use of false information that might mislead the consumer regarding the geographical origin, quality or properties of the product, and is put on the packing, business identification documents or other documents, which makes wrong impression for the real origin, and (5) another application which might mislead the consumer regarding the geographical origin of the product.[270]

§7. Limitations of the Scope of Protection

613. The authorized users of protected geographical names may not request prohibition due to infringement of the right when the geographical name is used for notification and education of the public in a way which is not harmful to their interests. The use of geographical names for these purposes is made without compensation.

§8. Duration of Protection

614. As far as the validity of the right is concerned, i.e., the duration of the protection, LIP prescribes that the protection of geographical name is indefinite, while using the protected geographical name shall be valid for five years from the date of adopting the decision. The validity of the right of use may be renewed an indefinite number of times for a period of five years provided that the right holder in the course of the fifth-year validity submits a request to SOIP for renewal of the right to use the protected geographical name. The right of using the protected geographical name will be renewed if the requirements for granting that right have been fulfilled; otherwise, the right shall cease to have effect on the date following the date of expiry of the fifth year of its validity.[271]

269. LIP, Art. 257.
270. LIP, Art. 259.
271. LIP, Art. 246.

615. The decision for granting the right of using the protected geographical name may be revoked if it is determined that the requirements for granting the right to use the protected geographical name ceased to have effect. In the procedure, on request for revoking the decision for granting of the right for using protected geographical name, the authorized user of the protected geographical name shall be bound to prove that there are requirements for granting of the right.[272] The decision for granting the right of using the protected geographical name may be revoked ex officio, or on the request of an interested entity or association (authorized to submit an application for registration of geographical name), as well as on a proposal from the public prosecutor. Evidence should be attached to the request for revoking a decision. Within fifteen days from the receipt of the revoking request, SOIP forwards it to the holder of the right to use and invites him to declare himself thereon within thirty days from the date of receiving the notification.[273] In case of decision for revoking, the right to use protected geographical name shall cease to have effect for the person registered as an authorized user in the appropriate registers the day following the date of the effective decision for revoking that right.[274]

616. A similar provision on revoking of the right to protected designation of origin and protected geographical indications for agricultural products is contained in LQAP. Namely, if the verification bodies determine that the production of an agricultural or food product is not in accordance with the conditions set out in the elaboration or specification, the Minister of Agriculture, Forestry and Water Economy (on the proposal of the special committee for applications) adopts a decision for deletion of the subject from the respective register.[275]

§9. Infringement and Remedies

617. Infringement of geographical indications and appellations of origin rights results in civil remedies and/or criminal sanctions. Furthermore, administrative law protection is provided through the supervision provided by the competent state organ as well as through the rules of the misdemeanour procedure. Concerning the civil remedies, any unauthorized use, availability, restriction, imitation, association, rights harassment, and the like contrary to the provisions of LIP is considered as infringement of the rights. Civil penalty is also prescribed in LIP, in the cases of infringement, no matter if done intentionally or with ultimate negligence. Regarding the interim measures, the court can order them when the plaintiff proposes them if he provides evidence that will prove that the right has been violated or will be violated. Regarding the criminal sanctions,[276] the CrC of

272. LIP, Art. 262.
273. *Ibid.*
274. LIP, Art. 264(2).
275. LQAP, Art. 153.
276. More on criminal law aspects of intellectual property in the Macedonian legislation in: Naumovski, G., Gruevska, A., Stefanovski, Lj. (2006) 'Krivično-pravna zaštita intelektualne svojine u Makedoniji', Pravni život, Časopis za pravnu teoriju i praksu, Kopaonička škola prirodnog prava Udruženja pravnika Srbije, 11/2006, p. 917–931.

Macedonia[277] prescribes sanctions in the case of violation of industrial property rights. Border measures are also part of the Macedonian legislation as stipulated by the Law on Customs Measures for the Protection of Intellectual Property Rights (LCM).[278] Considering the administrative law protection, LIP prescribes supervision by the State Market Inspectorate.

§10. Overlapping and Relation to Other Intellectual Property Laws

618. Having in mind the dispersed approach of geographical indications and appellation of origin regulations in the LIP,[279] LQAP,[280] and Law on Wine,[281] it would be crucial to develop a more consistent legal framework that would foster the benefits of the use of geographical indications and applications of origin for all sectors.

277. *See* Criminal Code, Art. 285, Official Journal of the Republic of Macedonia Nos 37/96, 80/99, 48/01, 4/02, 16/02, 43/03, 19/04, 40/2004, 81/05, 50/06, 60/06, 373/06, 87/07, 7/08, 139/08, 114/09, 51/11-3, 51/11-79, 135/11, 185/11, 142/12, 143/12 166/12, 55/13, 82/13, 14/14, 27/14, 28/14, 41/14, 115/14, 132/14, 160/14, 199/14, 196/15, 226/15, 7/17, 170/17, 248/18.
278. Official Journal of the Republic of Macedonia, 88/15, 154/15, 192/15, 23/16, 110/21.
279. Official Journal Nos 21/09, 24/11, 12/14, 41/14, 152/15, 53/16, 83/18, 31/20.
280. Official Journal Nos 140/10, 53/11, 55/12, 106/13, 116/15, 149/15, 193/15, 39/16.
281. Official Journal Nos 50/10, 53/11, 6/12, 23/13, 106/13, 188/13, 149/15, 39/16, 172/16.

Selected Bibliography

Books (Monographs)

Reboul, Y., Polenak Akimovska, M. & Naumovski G. *Introduction to Trademarks and Geographical Indications*. Tempus project 144582. Skopje: Faculty of Law Iustinianus Primus, 2010.

Articles

Buchkovski, V., Gavrilovikj N., Naumovski G. & Vuchen F. Geographical Indications Protection in the Republic of Macedonia with reference to wines. Intellectual Property, Innovation and Science in A Global Environment-. Collection with Papers of the Fifth National Seminar with International Participation, Sofia, 2017 (pp. 41–52): University of Library Studies and Information Technologies, University Youth Knowledge Academy, Sofia, 2017.

Bugaj, U. et al. Archaeological, Topographical and Geophysical Research on the Neolithic Tells in Pelagonia. *Sprawozdania Archeologiczne*, 66 (2014): 221–240.

Kambovska, M. Avtorskoto pravo vo vo Evropskata unija I vo Republika Makedonija: Predizvici vo Digitalnoto Opkruzuvanje [Copyright Law in the European Union and in the Republic of Macedonia: Challenges in the Digital Environment]. Doctoral Dissertation, Iustinianus Primus Law Faculty Skopje, 2010.

Kambovska, M. Regulation of online Platforms: EU policy and its reflection on policies in the Republic of North Macedonia, 2020. Available online: https://dijalogkoneu.mk/en/wp-content/uploads/sites/3/2020/10/Regulation-of-online-Platforms-1.pdf.

Naumovski, G. Geographical Indications in Macedonian Law. *WIPO-WTO Papers*, 1 (2010): 69–80.

Naumovski, G., Gruevska, A. & Stefanovski, Lj. Krivično-pravna zaštita intelektualne svojine u Makedoniji [Criminal Law Protection of Intellectual Property in Macedonia. In Serbian]. *Pravni život, Časopis za pravnu teoriju i praksu*, 11 (2006): 917–931.

Šalamanov-Korobar, L. Analysis of Chipped Stone Artifacts from Middle Paleolithic Lazers in the Cave Golema Pešt. *Macedoniae Acta Archaelogica*, 21 (2019): 1–538.

Selected Bibliography

Index

The numbers here refer to paragraph numbers.

Index

www.ingramcontent.com/pod-product-compliance
Ingram Content Group UK Ltd.
Pitfield, Milton Keynes, MK11 3LW, UK
UKHW020145290926
15471UKWH00004B/711

9 789403 507866